Making
Innovation
Happen

THE SUNDAY TIMES

Making Innovation Happen

Michael Morgan

△△△ KOGAN PAGE | *CREATING SUCCESS*

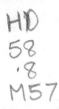

HD
58
·8
M57

Published in Australia by Business + Publishing, Warriewood, Australia, 2000
First published in the UK by Kogan Page, 2001

Kogan Page Limited
120 Pentonville Road
London N1 9JN

The views expressed in this book are those of the author, and are not necessarily the same as those of Times Newspapers Ltd.

British Library Cataloguing in Publication Data

A CIP record for this book is available from the British Library.

ISBN 0 7494 3432 5

Typeset by Jean Cussons Typesetting, Diss, Norfolk
Printed and bound in Great Britain by Clays Ltd, St Ives plc

contents

about the author

Michael Morgan is CEO of Herrmann International Asia, an international company specialising in creativity, innovation and thinking in business. He has had over 15 years of experience in helping people and organisations become more creative and innovative, working with companies like Boral Ltd, DBSLAND (Singapore), Ericsson Australia, Honeywell Ltd, the Macquarie Graduate School of Management and the Singapore Civil Service.

Michael is the author of *Creating Workforce Innovation* (1993, Business & Professional Publishing, Sydney, Australia) and is an internationally acclaimed speaker and presenter. He was one of four international speakers at the Taiwan Government's Human Resource Conference in 1999 and also spoke at the seventh International Conference on Thinking in Singapore. He runs programmes in Hong Kong and Singapore regularly, and has spoken recently to groups in Austria, Australia, Malaysia, New Zealand and Thailand.

For information on Herrmann International Asia, and to contact the author, please visit www.herrmann.com.au.

introduction

Innovation is more than a good idea. Innovation is the process that takes a good idea, improves it, develops it and implements it.

Most businesses are not short of ideas. What they are short of is the ability to innovate. Many businesses find it difficult to take those ideas and do something with them, quickly and effectively. Many businesses find innovation difficult.

It is one thing to have an idea. It is something different to take that idea and develop it into something that a business can market or sell. *Making Innovation Happen* describes the four key elements that are essential for any business to sustain innovation:

- The first key element is Purpose. Innovative companies have developed a common purpose shared by everyone.
- The second key element is Commitment. Innovative companies have demonstrated that they are totally committed to innovation and all that it involves.
- The third key element is Ideas. Innovative companies encourage and welcome ideas. They train people in creative thinking skills and allow people time to think.

■ The fourth key element is Support. Innovative companies understand that ideas and the people who have
them need support. They need policies and procedures
that work for them, not against them. They need the
moral and financial support needed to take an idea
from concept to finished product.

Making Innovation Happen shows how easy it is to turn
almost any business into an innovative business.

introducing innovation

- innovation and juggling;
- key elements of sustained innovation;
- making innovation happen;
- benefits of the innovative organisation.

There is a lot more to juggling than throwing three balls in the air and trying to catch them. Juggling involves keeping your eyes on more than one thing at a time. It means moving continuously and quickly while making slight adjustments in the way you catch or throw the balls. It involves watching, moving, responding, adjusting, catching, throwing and concentrating. It also requires you to let things go. Juggling is dynamic. Juggle and you will never feel totally in control.

innovation and juggling

Innovation is like juggling; see Figure 1.1. Simply throwing some ideas in the air and seeing what happens to them will not work. Like juggling, innovation involves keeping your eyes on more than one thing at a time while moving continuously and quickly. It involves making slight adjustments in the way you do things, always watching, moving, responding, adjusting, catching, throwing and concentrating – and letting things go.

Innovation is as dynamic as juggling. Innovate and you will never feel totally in control.

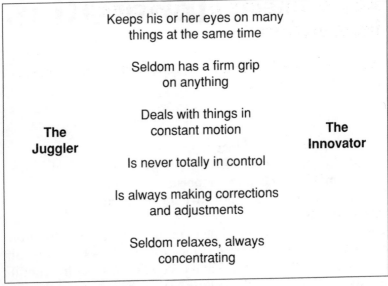

The Juggler

Keeps his or her eyes on many things at the same time

Seldom has a firm grip on anything

Deals with things in constant motion

Is never totally in control

Is always making corrections and adjustments

Seldom relaxes, always concentrating

The Innovator

Figure 1.1   *Innovation and juggling*

People seem to juggle with almost anything. Balls, bats, knives and even chainsaws get thrown around to demonstrate their skills and to distinguish themselves from others. People often think that, just as juggling and innovation share some important skills, innovation and juggling can both work with random 'objects'. Grab anything, throw it up in the air and let's see what happens. Something innovative will happen as a result. Well, something innovative *might* happen as a result, but it will be pure luck.

Innovation, especially sustained or purposeful innovation, requires that you juggle with the right things. Throw the wrong things in the air and you could end up with anything, or nothing. Throw the right things in the air and you end up with sustained innovation.

key elements of sustained innovation

What are the right things to juggle with in the innovation process? They are:

- purpose;
- commitment;
- ideas;
- support.

purpose

Everyone wants to get something out of life. Every company wants to achieve certain things. In innovative companies the people and the organisation are all trying to achieve similar things. They are all going in the same direction. There is a common purpose. Boats, for example, don't get very far if everyone is rowing in different directions.

Whenever I work with a group of people from a single organisation, I always ask what the organisation's purpose is. In most cases, you would think everyone worked for different organisations! Everyone comes up with a different statement, and those who get it right usually do so because they pull out the credit-card-sized memory jogger with the organisational aim or mission statement printed on it.

While it is rare to get everyone to know and understand what the organisation's purpose is, it is still a vital ingredient in the innovation process. Innovation demands a common purpose.

commitment

Most companies are not short of ideas. What they are short of, however, is the commitment of people to lend their weight, to help and support those ideas. Commitment is showing your support for something. Commitment is what people actually do each and every day. It is the little things as well as the big things they do. It is listening to ideas, taking time with people, offering assistance, overcoming barriers, encouraging people and being true to your word. Commitment is saying you are going to do something and then doing it. Commitment is how you behave.

For innovation to become a way of life, people need to show their commitment at every level of the organisation. One of the best examples of commitment I have ever seen was from Chris Johns.

commitment from the top

Chris was the CEO of a retail clothing company. The company had a network of retail outlets in large shopping centres across Australia. Chris wanted these stores to stand out more. He wanted his staff to be more creative in the way they presented their stock and managed the shops. So he asked me to run a series of Creative Thinking Workshops.

Chris sat in on the first workshop to see how it went. Sitting in his office after the workshop, he asked me if I would train him to run the workshops. He said his job as CEO was to have the biggest possible impact on the company that he possibly could. He felt he could not achieve that by sitting in his office. He thought the best way to do it was to actually go and run the creative thinking workshops himself. And this is exactly what he did.

He designed a workshop that did two things. It taught people a variety of creative thinking skills, and it showed them how to use those skills at work. For example, with each new product release, each store received a 'marketing kit' to go with it. Instead of just opening the marketing kit and setting it up, he showed people how to use it and adapt it to fit their specific needs. He told them to look at what other stores were doing and to use their ideas as well. He encouraged them to make their store the best looking store in the complex.

The workshops achieved two things. Their stores were often voted the 'best looking store' in many shopping centres and, perhaps more importantly, Chris had empowered the people in each store to take the initiative and implement their ideas.

Chris's commitment to creative thinking and innovation was there for everyone to see. Innovation needs such commitment.

ideas

Innovation requires people to think in different ways. It needs people who are good at analysis and problem solving. It needs people who are good at coming up with ideas and following hunches. It needs people who are good at implementing ideas and getting things done.

In one company I worked with, over 100 people were trained in creative thinking. They were all involved in new product development. This company wanted a constant stream of new products coming onto the market. Training their people in the many aspects of product development and creative thinking was a vital part of this highly successful strategy. Innovation needs ideas.

support

For an organisation to become innovative, you need to get everyone involved. To get everyone involved, innovation needs to be built in to the way people work day to day. People need a support structure to make it happen. They need an organisation that is structured in a way that encourages and develops ideas. They need policies that encourage ideas. They need procedures that help them develop their ideas. They need systems in place that make it easy to implement ideas.

One IT company I worked with created a number of special 'innovation positions'. The top position was Director of Innovation. That job was to guide the overall innovation process and to implement policies and procedures that supported innovation. In each department they created the position of Innovation Champion. The Champion's job was to provide ongoing help and support to anyone who needed it – to support ideas as they made their way through the ideas selection process. Innovation needs such support.

In *Making Innovation Happen*, we will look at purpose, commitment, ideas and support in turn. We will see what each one means, what each one involves and how you can actually get them happening in your organisation. We will see what other innovators have done. We will see how to juggle with all four key elements at the same time and keep them all 'up in the air'.

making innovation happen

Making Innovation Happen is a book designed to help you to introduce innovation to your work area. Whether you are the CEO of a company, the manager of a project team or the supervisor or team leader of a work unit, you'll find plenty of practical ideas and processes you can implement yourself. It will show you not only how to be innovative yourself, but also how to involve other people and other teams.

Chapter 2, How Innovation Works, looks at ideas and where they come from. Different types of innovation are examined.

We see how, often by just changing your perspective, you can be more innovative. It also shows how 'small' ideas can be just as innovative as big ones.

Chapter 3, Getting Innovation Started, covers how to start juggling. The first three issues you need to juggle with – purpose, commitment and ideas – are introduced here. In each case, you'll find specific ideas and processes you can implement to help make you, your people and the teams they work in become more innovative. You'll also find lots of examples of what some of the most innovative organisations have done.

Chapter 4, Juggling Support, is all about supporting the jugglers. Creating the right environment needed for innovation to flourish is vital, and in Chapter 4 you find out how. This chapter has examples of what organisations have actually done and the resources they have provided to make innovation work.

Chapter 5, Tools of the Trade, is your toolkit. It is a collection of activities, worksheets and checklists that you can use immediately – either on your own, or as part of a team approach to innovation. At each stage of your journey to innovation, you'll be directed to the appropriate activities and worksheets in Chapter 5.

Making Innovation Happen is a practical book, full of proven ideas, tools and techniques that can help turn any workplace into an innovative workplace.

benefits of the innovative organisation

I remember my first real experience with ideas and organisations. It was all about this idea I had. I knew it was a winner. My problem was to convince 'the powers that be' that it was. The 'powers that be' were all in head office. All I could do was to put my idea through the normal 'idea scheme' and wait for an answer.

At the time, I was working with a government department. My idea was simple enough – to put on a 'dairy display' at the local agricultural show. We could hire a pavilion and fill it full of cows, milking machines and dairy products. We could then run a series of talks and demonstrations to entertain and educate people during the show. I thought it would enhance the image of the department – we could disseminate lots of information and it would help us build relationships with the rural community. It was a great idea.

Needless to say, I ran straight into resistance. When I eventually did get a reply from head office, I got the usual barrage of objections. I was told, 'It won't work', 'It's too expensive', 'No one will come', 'We tried it once before' and 'We can't afford it'. What really annoyed me about these comments was that they were coming from people far removed from the action. They were all in 'head office' and had little or no idea about what I was actually talking about. I remember becoming really dispirited and demotivated. I felt like giving up. It was then that Ben Hall walked into my office. Ben was the Regional Manager and was in charge of things locally. He had heard about my idea and wanted to know more. So I told him about the idea and what I wanted to do. He liked it. He even made some suggestions to improve it. He said he would not only support it, but would also provide the money needed to make it happen.

With Ben Hall's support and encouragement, the idea suddenly took off. I got ideas and offers of support from everywhere. People joined in and made suggestions. What had begun as one person with one idea soon became an innovative project involving everyone. What had begun as an idea for a dairy display had grown into an exhibition of 'The latest trends in agriculture'.

When the show opened, so did we. We had a huge marquee full of the latest and greatest in agriculture. We had cows being milked, pigs being fed, butter being made and sheep being shorn. We had pictures, brochures, talks and videos all going on at once. We were never without a queue of people waiting to come in. We were voted the best and the most popular display at the show. And that was only the first year. When show time came around the following year, we were there again, bigger and better than the year before.

This story illustrates some of the benefits of innovation. It is a great example of how everyone can win through innovation. I won because an idea I had was taken seriously and implemented. Others won because they became part of it and helped it grow. Ben Hall won because he created a highly motivated and productive team. The local show won because of the high quality display. The people won as they walked in and saw what we had created. And finally, the organisation won because it enhanced its image with the rural community.

Making Innovation Happen can help everyone in your organisation win.

how innovation works

- the creativity zone;
- the four Ps of innovation;
- changing the course of history;
- more than just a good idea.

the creativity zone

Where are you when you get your best ideas? What do all those places have in common?

When people ask me about innovation, this is one of the first questions I ask. And when I do, most people say they get their best ideas 'in the shower'! The next most popular answer is 'on the toilet', followed by 'in bed', 'jogging', 'walking', 'exercising', 'gardening' and 'relaxing'.

In explaining what these places have in common, the most popular answer is 'relaxing', followed by 'quiet', 'peaceful', 'alone', 'not thinking about anything in particular', 'letting go', 'not stressful', 'doing something different', 'doing something physical' and 'dreaming'.

So, if you want your organisation to be more innovative and the people in it to have a million and one positive ideas, this conjures up some interesting pictures of what the workplace might have to look like!

What do most organisations actually look like? What environment do most people work in? What is the environment that *you* work in like?

Most people describe the environment they work in as busy, with no time to think, stressful, full of noise, nothing but deadlines, rushed, full of people, hectic, pressured and so on. Business today creates environments that sometimes make it hard to think, let alone to relax. We live in a competitive, high-tech world where speed and responsiveness are vital. We want people to be full of ideas and yet we often make it very difficult for them to have any. We want innovation and yet we make it almost impossible.

Most people think of innovation as purely product innovation. What we need to do is think of innovation in a broader way. We need to think of innovation as perhaps resulting in product innovation but beginning with other types of innovation. If you want innovative products, the first thing to do is to create an environment in which it can happen. If you provide an environment that encourages people to think and have ideas, innovation will follow. Get the environment right and people will have no trouble coming up with a stream of innovative products. Get the environment wrong and nothing will happen.

As we will see, juggling innovation is all about creating the right environment. Juggling is more than encouraging people to come up with a million and one ideas. Juggling is enabling people to turn those ideas into reality. That is what innovation is really all about.

the four Ps of innovation

How innovative are you now? Are people in your organisation

or team able to think and have ideas? Can people work on their ideas? Are people able to develop them and implement them?

Ask yourself, 'What innovations, of any kind, have been introduced or implemented in the last 12 months?' To help answer this question, try thinking about the four Ps of innovation:

1. procedural innovation;
2. people innovation;
3. process innovation;
4. product innovation.

1. procedural innovation

Procedural innovation refers to improvements in how the business operates internally. It might include changes to accounting procedures, purchasing and stock control, internal communication systems, payroll procedures and office layout and design.

Examples are using the Internet and tele-banking to cut down on the number of cheques written; computerised stock control and re-ordering systems to cut down on inventory; e-mail and intranet facilities to speed up communication and creative use of office space to encourage free thinking.

---

improvements in communication

In our organisation we produce a monthly newsletter for our clients. We used to print out 500 copies of the newsletter each month, print the mailing labels, stick them on the envelopes, stuff the envelopes, sort them into postcodes, take them to the post office and write a cheque to cover the postage. This took one person up to a day to do. Now I attach the newsletter to an e-mail and send it automatically. It takes me less than a minute.

2. people innovation

Innovation can affect the ways people in your organisation work together – cross-functional teams, virtual teams, reward and incentive schemes, pay structures and promotional policies are all areas in which 'people innovation' can be made.

For example, innovation might create project teams with representatives from across the organisation, intranet-based teams across international boundaries, an incentive scheme that pays people for their ideas or dual career ladders.

---

the international author network

I am part of a network of business consultants. We are spread across Asia from Melbourne to Tokyo. Kris, based in Bangkok, suggested that between us we could write a book. We agreed on a structure, we all wrote a chapter and e-mailed it to each other for editing and comments. Within four months, we had a 250-page book ready to go. It was a great example of a virtual team creating a book in a very innovative way.

---

3. process innovation

'Process' is how the product is produced and how it reaches the customer, from manufacturing to marketing. Examples of process innovation are increased efficiency, simplified and streamlined operations, new marketing and positioning campaigns and process re-engineering.

Coca-Cola is not famous for the number of products it has. The world really only knows about one of its products – Coke. What Coca-Cola is brilliant at is marketing. It is brilliant at positioning Coke in the mind of the customer, in promoting it and distributing it. Almost every day you see a new advert for Coke, a new-look vending machine or a new place where you can buy the product. If you want to know how to position a product, look no further than Coke.

McDonalds is another example of effective process innovation. Its ability to get a standardised product to the customer in almost every corner of the world is legendary. McDonalds is a model of distribution, of positioning, of processes that deliver a guaranteed product to the customer every time.

using the Internet for process innovation

We have a product called the HBDI (the Herrmann Brain Dominance Instrument), which is a 120-question survey that measures people's 'thinking preferences'. Individuals fill in the form and return it to us for processing. Processing involves checking the forms to ensure that they are filled in correctly and returning them if necessary. It then involves data entry, printing, collating, assembly and finally dispatch back to the person concerned. This process used to be all done on paper and involved a lot of data entry and handling. We had a continuous stream of couriers picking up and delivering forms at our Sydney office.

The process worked well enough when all our business came from the Sydney market. It did not work well as we tried to expand into overseas markets. We needed to radically change the way we processed these forms. We did so by developing an Internet-based software program that enabled the person filling in the form in the first place to do it online. Using the Web browser, they filled in the form and pressed the 'submit' button. The data from their form was immediately sent to our server.

This simple process reduced the overall processing time by up to six days, it made it more cost-effective and reduced the number of data entry errors by almost 100 per cent. It also allowed us to expand our market dramatically. With the original paper-based process, our business was restricted to Australia. We now do business across Asia into China and Korea and as far west as the United Arab Emirates.

4. product innovation

Products are what customers actually buy. Examples of product innovation are product enhancements, product redesign and new product development.

3M is famous for its ability to get new and exciting products to market. Think of 3M and most people think of the Post-it note and adhesive tape. Sony is another company that is always launching yet another innovative product. The original Walkman, the Video Walkman, the MiniDisc and the Jogger Player are some of the hundreds of Sony products you can now buy.

One of the most recent product innovations is also to do with our product, the HBDI. Participants used to receive their results in the form of a full colour profile printed on paper and a workbook that explained it in detail. They would look at the profile and read the workbook. Now they receive their profile printed not on paper but on a transparency. They also receive four different workbooks instead of just one. Each workbook is designed to be interactive. Using the transparency as an overlay, the participant now works through a series of exercises in each of the workbooks. What was a passive learning exercise is now a highly interactive one.

Recently I ran an exercise with a group of 24 managers from a large construction company. I asked them to use the four Ps to categorise any innovations introduced in the last four years. Ninety per cent turned out to be product innovations; 10 per cent were process innovations. No one could come up with an example of a procedural or people innovation.

Innovative organisations that have the right environment tend to be good at all types of innovation. The environment enables people in all parts of the organisation to be innovative. From the research and development department to the sales department, from accounting to warehousing, the right environment allows innovation to occur. Truly innovative companies are innovative in many different ways.

tools of the trade

Refer to Activity 1 on page 104 and Worksheet 1 on page 105 for The Four Ps. Try completing the activity with your organisation in mind.

What does it tell you about the opportunities for innovation within your organisation? Use it with a group or team and get them involved.

changing the course of history

The invention of the wheel changed the course of history. The Wright brothers, Edison, Archimedes, Aristotle, John Lennon and Gandhi all had ideas that have left their marks on history. Other people have created great symphonies, written novels, made epic films and done things that have affected the lives of millions.

I have had a few good ideas but none of them has changed the course of history. The biggest idea I ever had was to climb Nelson's Column in London. I was a student at the time and a group of us climbed to the top. No one ever believed we had done it! So much for that idea.

Most of my ideas since then have been quite small. I worked out a way to stop the skylight from leaking, I solved a problem with the pool filter, I managed to keep a demanding customer happy and I cooked a great fish dish the other night. I even had a great idea for a marketing brochure. Time will tell how good it was. I also have lots of other ideas: about this boat I want, about driving around Australia, about this new Internet-based product, about how to get more business and so on.

What sort of ideas have you come up with? Have you changed the course of history? Perhaps not. You are probably more like me. You have had lots of small ideas. Having small ideas is just as good as having big ideas. Ideas, whatever the size, are the starting point of innovation. They are vital to the process.

the triple jump of innovation

The triple jump involves trying to cover as much distance as you can, first with a hop, then with a bigger step, followed by an enormous jump. Innovation is the same. You are trying to put as much distance as you can between you and the competition. You are trying to come up with as many innovations as you can – innovations that can hop, step or jump!

innovations that hop

Innovations that hop are small innovations that happen every day and often go unnoticed. They are innovations like a new way to make a sauce, to cut meat, to fold a letter, to water plants, to hit the ball, to undo the screw, to fill in the form, to beat the rain.

innovations that step

These are innovations that people take notice of. They are ideas like getting cash at the supermarket till, having a television in every seat on the plane, creating a new customer service strategy, a new procedure, a new way of washing cars.

ideas that jump

These are the innovations that change the world, turn industries upside down, alter lives and affect a lot of people. These innovations are like inventing a breakthrough computer chip, composing a mighty symphony, emigrating and starting a new life or building your own business.

Certain companies excel at a certain kinds of innovation and struggle to come to terms with others. They might be good at product innovation but not so good at process innovation. We have also seen how some companies are born out of a great idea but find it hard to repeat it, while others continue with small everyday innovations that add up to continued success. As the world we work in becomes more chaotic and competitive, we need every kind of innovation we can get, in every part of the organisation.

tools of the trade

Refer to Activity 2, The Triple Jump, on page 106. Try completing it with your organisation in mind. What does it tell you about the opportunities for innovation within your organisation? Try it with a group or team and involve them in the hunt for innovation.

Refer to Activity 3 on page 108. It's a great way to find where the opportunities for innovation really do exist.

more than just a good idea

Competition is getting tougher everyday. Someone, somewhere, is tempting your clients with a better deal, a lower price, a quicker service, an alternative product, a new way, a faster way or a different way. If organisations are to stay in business, they have to look at every part of what they do and find new and innovative ways of operating. They need to innovate everywhere. They need innovative products, innovative ways of delivering those products, innovative ways of positioning those products, innovative ways of gaining new markets and protecting existing ones and innovative ways of operating internally and keeping track of everything. They need procedural, people, process and product innovation. And they need ideas of all sizes.

The question is not so much, 'Should we innovate?' but, 'Where should we start?'. I believe the place to start is with the organisation itself. Start by asking the questions:

- ■ How can we make this a more innovative place to work?
- ■ How can we help people to think more and to have more ideas?

■ How can we help people to work on their ideas?
■ How can we help people to develop their ideas and to implement them?

Juggling is the only way to answer these questions. It is the only way to create an innovative environment.

getting innovation started

■ juggling innovation;
■ juggling purpose;
■ juggling commitment;
■ juggling ideas;
■ The IDEA process.

juggling innovation

We have already talked about innovation as being something complex and ever changing. There are no magical steps to follow. There is no one secret formula that will guarantee success, no simple recipe. Rather, innovation is something that is continually happening and always moving. It is a highly dynamic process. We have also discovered that innovation is a lot more than just creating and marketing new products. Innovation is important to every part of the organisation. Innovation is about ideas, big and small. It is as important in the way you work with people as it is in what they produce. In any organisation there are many opportunities to benefit from innovation.

The real challenge of innovation is how to create a culture and environment that encourages the natural creativity in everyone. How can you create an organisation that motivates everyone and enables him or her to contribute to the future of the organisation? Do that and you really will have an innovative organisation.

To create such an organisation you need to be good at juggling four things. They are:

▓ purpose;
▓ commitment;
▓ ideas;
▓ support.

what does juggling mean in the innovation process?

Everyone wants to get something out of life. Every company wants to achieve certain things. In innovative companies the people and the company are all trying to achieve similar things. They are all going in the same direction. There is a common purpose. Boats, for example, don't get very far if everyone is rowing in different directions. Juggling is about developing a common purpose.

Most companies are not short of ideas. What they are short of is the commitment of others to lend their weight, to help and support the ideas of others. There are often too many obstacles to overcome along the way. Total commitment at all levels by all concerned is needed if innovation is to become a way of life. Juggling is about showing commitment and helping to over-come obstacles.

Innovation requires people to think in different ways. It needs people who are good at analysis and problem solving. It needs people who are good at coming up with ideas and following hunches. It needs people who are good at implementing ideas and getting things done. Juggling is about having and implementing ideas.

For an organisation to become innovative, everyone has to be involved. For everyone to be involved, innovation must be a part of everyday life. Policies, procedures, systems and rewards need to be in place so that everyone can naturally use their heads and be innovative. Innovation will fail if it is left to the 'creative few'. Juggling is about providing this support.

The rest of this chapter examines in more detail the first three of these four critical success factors – purpose, commitment and ideas – and explains how to juggle with the three of them at the same time. The issue of support is covered in Chapter 4.

juggling purpose

Have you ever seen a dragon boat race? It looks as if everyone is paddling his or her own canoe. There is a lot of noise and splashing. A drummer beats out the time while everyone else in the boat paddles like mad towards the finishing line. In spite of how it looks, most of the time they have their act together. They are all facing the same way. They have a drummer beating the time and they all know what they are trying to do.

A Formula 1 racing team is similar. From the outside it often looks chaotic and hectic and yet inside people are focused and clear about what they are trying to do. Ask any member of an orchestra what they are doing and why, and they will tell you. Stay awake during an operation and you will see another team performing well. A surgical team also knows what it is doing and why.

In each case individuals come together to achieve something. In each case they know what it is they are trying to achieve and why they are doing it. They have a common goal and, despite any differences there might be between individuals in the team, they all work together to achieve that goal.

what are you trying to do?

Getting an organisation, or group of people within an organisation, to be more innovative is similar. They need to know what it is they are trying to achieve, and most importantly, why. Dragon boat racing and F1 racing are about winning. Playing in an orchestra is about the performance and getting it right. Surgery is about healing and wellbeing.

What is it you want your people to do? What is it you want them to achieve?

I'm helping put a man on the moon

A consultant was visiting the NASA-Kennedy Space Center in the early 1970s. During his inspection he found himself in the amenities block, a large building containing the canteen, the showers and toilets. He stopped to talk to a man in an official-looking pair of blue NASA overalls.

The consultant asked, 'And what do you do here?' The man replied, 'I'm helping put a man on the moon.'

The man was the janitor, responsible for cleaning the showers and toilets. How does a janitor help put a man on the moon? Well, imagine that you are an astronaut. You have had a bad day, doing weightlessness training all day. You have been upside down, spun around and pushed around. All you want to do is get out of the heavy boots and the funny hat and go home. You arrive at the amenities block to find no soap, dirty towels and a far-from-nice smell in the air. How do you feel? What does it do to your motivation? How do you feel about the moon?

Imagine, on the other hand, that everything was sparkling and clean, that there was a freshness in the air and the soap was where it should be. What effect would it have on your motivation?

The man in the overalls was just one of many. He was an individual who could have easily been forgotten in the grand scheme of things. He was an individual who could have been given a job to do with little or no explanation as to its value and contribution.

If all you want is an organisation full of people who just do the job and nothing more, then perhaps overlooking the importance of every individual to the aims of the organisation is OK. If you want a company that is innovative, if you want people to get involved in this messy process called innovation and contribute ideas and energy, then you need to provide more. You need to provide meaning. You need to provide a clear purpose.

doing things on purpose

Profit is like oxygen, food and water for the body. They are not the meaning of life but without them there is no life.

I don't know who said that, but it's true. I know a lot of organisations that have had things like 'Maximise shareholder value', 'Maximise before-tax profits' and 'Increase return on investments' as goals. The only people who will be the slightest bit interested in those are the shareholders, the CEO (whose very job depends upon achieving them) and anyone else who might share in the profit. For most of the people who work in the organisation they are meaningless aims and provide little or no motivation. Sometimes they can actually demotivate employees and work against you.

Organisations need to make money. We all know that. They would not be in business if they didn't. So let's take that as a given and move beyond it.

Herrmann International, my organisation, provides consulting skills and training tools for business. We help individuals and companies improve the way they 'think'. Naturally, I want the business to make money. But beyond that, our real purpose is to 'Create better business through better thinking'. If we can do that, we might even be able to 'Create a better world through better thinking' – and *that* is exciting. If we could help solve some of the problems that the world is facing, I think we would have achieved a lot. That is what we are about. That is what we are trying to achieve.

Innovation is very important to us. I want Herrmann International to be a highly innovative company. I am hoping that our purpose of 'Creating better business through better thinking' will encourage everyone to be more innovative and to try exciting things – both for us and for our clients.

3M drives innovation with the statement: 'Our real business is solving problems'. American Express wants to provide 'Heroic customer service'. Boeing wants to be 'On the leading edge of aeronautics, being pioneers'. Johnson and Johnson exists to 'Alleviate pain and suffering'. Disney seeks 'Continuous progress through creativity, dreams and imagination' and Sony wants to 'Be a pioneer, not by following others but by doing the impossible'.

Does your organisation have a clear sense of purpose?

a clear sense of purpose

A clear sense of purpose is:

- simple;
- memorable;
- magic;
- for everyone.

For your purpose to be simple, it must be a few words that are clear, straightforward and unambiguous. 'Our real business is solving problems' gets straight to the point.

For your purpose to be memorable, it should be something you don't have to look up or write down, like 'Helping put a man on the moon'. A good statement of purpose has to hook people emotionally. 'Heroic customer service' has magic.

Make your purpose a statement that unites everyone: 'On the leading edge of aeronautics, being pioneers' works for the CEO *and* the design engineer.

developing organisational purpose

Organisational purpose is nothing more than a clear statement about what the organisation is doing and why. To develop this clear statement, simply ask the right questions and keep asking them till you get the answer you want. The question to ask is always the same – 'Why?'. Why are we doing what we are doing? Ask 'why' enough times and you will get the answer. Five times usually seems to get you there. An example follows.

developing a purpose for Herrmann International

Why No. 1: Why does Herrmann International exist?
It exists to make money and to sell consulting services.
Why No. 2: Why?
It wants to make money so it can pay its people. It wants to sell consulting services because they are very good and can make a difference.
Why No. 3: Why?
They are very good because they are well researched and deal with how people think. They make a difference because they improve the way people think, learn and make decisions.
Why No. 4: Why?
Thinking is something we all do every day. Yet sometimes we are not very good at it. In the world today there are plenty of examples of the results of poor thinking and decision making.
Why No. 5: Why?
It took us 12 months to get the wording right, but for us the answer was that our purpose is: 'To create a better world through better thinking'. More specifically, 'To create better business through better thinking'.

And we think that our statement of purpose is simple, memorable, magic and for everyone in Herrmann International.

I have worked with lots of organisations to help clarify their purpose. I remember one building company started with 'Increasing shareholder value' and ended up with 'Helping people build dreams'. Another construction company moved from 'Being the most profitable and first thought of' to 'Creating environments where others can excel'. Recently, I worked with the entire top team of a marketing company for three days to define their purpose. They now have a very clear purpose that is driving innovation for the next five years. What is exciting them already is that they are ahead of schedule and have achieved more in the last six months than they had in the previous three years. Having a clear purpose is critical to success.

tools of the trade

Refer to Activity 4, Organisational Purpose, on pages 110–11.

Try completing it with your organisation in mind. It will help clarify and develop a sense of organisational purpose.

juggling purpose

Purpose is the first of the four critical success factors for creating an innovative organisation. Everyone needs a reason to get up in the morning, a reason to come to work. Everyone needs to know what the organisation is trying to do and why. Purpose can provide that reason.

Ask people what the purpose of their organisation is and it's amazing how many pull out their wallets from their back pockets as if it's OK if you can't remember it, so long as you sit on it. That approach does not work too well. Purpose needs to be in their heads, not in their pockets.

Asking 'why' is the best way to develop purpose. Just keep asking and asking till you get beneath the surface and away from words like 'profit' and 'money'. Those things might keep the organisation in business, but they are not what drive the people in the business.

Finally, you need to keep your eye on the purpose all the time. You need to keep throwing it up in the air. You need to keep catching it. It will move around, it will change, it will take a slightly different path each time. It also does not have to be the first of the critical success factors you deal with, as long as you eventually do re-examine it.

The next critical success factor we will juggle with is showing your commitment to innovation.

juggling commitment

Gone are the days when you could command the cavalry charge from the safety of the ridge, gone the days when you can sit back and watch it all happen from a safe distance. Nowadays, you have to lead from the front. If you say 'Charge!', people will wait to see where you are. If you are standing on the ridge watching, don't expect everyone to charge off into the distance without you.

leading the charge

One of the most challenging workshops I ever ran was opened by a manager who said 'Charge!' and promptly left. That is, he spent the first 10 minutes telling the participants that this programme was especially for them, that he had tried everything else but nothing had worked, that they needed these skills and that if they didn't learn them they may as well look for another job. The skills he was talking about were the leadership skills of gaining commitment. Needless to say, when he left the room, it was full of totally uncommitted people. It was a clear example of the negative effects of saying 'charge' and then standing back to watch. He showed no commitment and got none in return.

Innovation is the cavalry charge of today. If you stand on the ridge watching, nothing much is going to happen. If you say 'charge' and leave the room, nothing will happen. You need to lead the charge. You need to be out there in front, leading the way. You need to be the first to be innovative. You need to stay in the room. That is the best way to show your commitment.

Four things you can do to lead the charge, to be out in front, to innovate and to show commitment are:

1. create thinking space;
2. climb the ladder;
3. ask 'What if...?';
4. give a little TLC.

Let's look more closely at each of them.

create thinking space

In Chapter 2 we noted the strange places people go to think and recognised how critical the environment is to thinking. It can either encourage it or stifle it. We all need space to think in.

We also discussed that the best place to start innovating is with the organisation itself. Here is a good chance to do just that. You can show your commitment by changing your working environment a bit. Create space to think in. This is something everyone will notice.

Start with your office. Think about where you are when you get your best ideas. Try and reproduce a bit of that special environment at work. Put some pictures on the wall, add a splash of colour, put some creative toys on the table, add a bit of background music, open the blinds, let the outside in and turn it into an office that really does encourage thinking. People will walk in and wonder what is going on. You can then tell them that innovation is becoming the way we do things here.

I read once that the human brain is hopeless at coming up with ideas. What it is good at is making connections. The richer the environment, the more the connections the brain will make and the more ideas you will end up with.

Have a go at any meeting rooms you have. Most meeting rooms do little to encourage thinking. They usually have white walls and venetian blinds. So put some pictures or posters on the walls, open up the blinds, replace all the black marker pens with coloured ones and throw a few toys and puzzles on the table. I know of two companies that did just this with their boardrooms. Now, instead of people just sitting there, barely listening as the energy level slowly drops, people doodle, play and fiddle. It sounds strange but it isn't. It actually works. Both companies have found that the meetings are more productive, people concentrate more and have many more ideas. Small changes can help people think and keep the mind active. It's well worth a try.

Once you have done this, encourage others to do the same. Make it a mission of yours to brighten up the entire office and create an environment that really is conducive to thinking.

the thinking area

One American company went even further. They decided that people needed two areas – one to work in and one to think in. So they gave everyone a workstation to work in, one that had phones, computers and all the other business tools needed for 'actual work'. They dedicated less than 50 per cent of the space available to these workstations. The rest of the area, more than half the office space, was dedicated to thinking. They filled it full of small informal sitting areas surrounded by plants. They provided a number of 'drink spots', complete with coffee and iced water. If you want to think on your own, or with a group of other people, you go to the thinking area. When you want to put your ideas to work, you go to the work area.

Do you have such a place where people can go to think things through? Is there a space where people can get away from it all for a few minutes and think about things? You can encourage people to think by creating a space that enables them to do so.

Try some small changes and additions and see what happens. If they work, keep going and try a few more things. Try it for a while and see what happens. People might start thinking more. And when you next ask the question, 'Where are you when you get your best ideas?', who knows, the answer might be, 'At work'!

climb the ladder

If you think about making your organisation more innovative, it is hard to know how or where to start. The challenge is almost too big. How can one person really make a difference? If you think about making one part of the organisation more innovative, it becomes a little more manageable. If you think about implementing just one or two ideas yourself, anything becomes possible.

Using 'the ladder' makes it easier to know where to start. The ladder will save you biting off more than you can chew and can reduce the risk of charging too far off into the distance before you find out if anyone is following. See Figure 3.1.

Top rung		How do I make the organisation more innovative?
One rung down		How do I make my division more innovative?
One rung down		How do I make my team more innovative?
One rung down		How can I be more innovative?
One rung down		How can I implement one new idea?

Figure 3.1 *The ladder*

What sort of view do you get from the top of a ladder? You can see a lot: you can look over things and down on things. You get the big picture. Climb down the ladder a bit and the view becomes more focused, more restricted and more detailed. Keep climbing down and you end up with your feet firmly on the ground.

Thinking about making the entire organisation more innovative is like being at the top of the ladder. Your view of the issues might be too high, too big and too complex. Coming down the ladder a bit and thinking about making your department more innovative might be a bit more manageable. Coming all the way down and implementing one innovative idea yourself might be more than possible.

Using the ladder will help determine the right place to start. You can think big and start at the top, or think smaller and start lower down. All you have to do is pick the right level to start on and give it a go.

Peter, the managing director of a small engineering company, uses the ladder as the starting point of all his problem-solving sessions. He says that better problem definition has helped him be more creative in the way his company solves problems.

tools of the trade
Refer to Activity 5, The Ladder, on page 113.

ask 'what if...?'
Remember the hop, step and jump? You could start your innovative charge with a huge jump and change the world forever. That is definitely starting at the top of the ladder. The other way to do it is to start with a few hops. It is sometimes better to get a few ideas hopping first, then move to some steps and finally to the big jump.

One good way to start hopping is to use a technique called 'What if...?'. You already use 'What if...?' every day. How many times have you asked yourself, 'What if it rains?', 'What if I'm late?' or 'What if I win?'? Most of us already use 'What if...?' to anticipate and prepare for all the everyday things we may face.

'What if...?' is a great technique to get people thinking and to get them started. Try adding it to any meeting agenda. In a sales meeting, spend five minutes thinking about the question, 'What if we got a new big client?' or 'What if we lost our biggest client?' In an office meeting, ask 'What if our computer network crashed?' or 'What if we automated the accounts system?'. In a strategy meeting, ask 'What if a new competitor came along?'. I even use it in sales calls. I ask it two ways: 'What if we do something?' and 'What if we don't do something?'. It's a great way to get people to think through the opportunities and consequences of a course of action.

You can use 'What if...?' for big and small issues. You can use 'What if...?' to solve real problems, anticipate new ones, stimulate thinking or just get people involved. Five minutes of 'What if...?' at any meeting shows everyone you are thinking, anticipating, open to ideas and willing to listen. 'What if...?' is a great way to show commitment. Who knows, something wonderful might come of it.

'what if...?' at work

One company I work with includes 'What if...?' sessions in all their meetings. They recently used it to anticipate what could happen if things went wrong with their new computer network. They were able to anticipate every malfunction and had a plan to deal with it.

I worked with another company that used 'What if...?' as the basis of their strategic planning process. They spent two days asking themselves, 'What if we did this?'. In one particular question they asked, 'What if we didn't have our new offices?'. Having spent the last two to three years designing them and setting them up, it was a brave question to ask. They talked about such things as working from home, using technology and leasing the office out. One stumbling block seemed to be the display area. Clients came in to look through the product display and make their selections. This was why they needed such large and appealing offices. The new office was something they could not do without. Or was it?

'What if' they had a virtual display centre? 'What if' they could put a laptop on the client's desk and show them everything there and then? The potential savings were enormous.

When I last spoke to this company, they were field-testing the virtual display centre and planning to introduce it across Australia.

tools of the trade

Refer to Activity 6, 'What if...?' on page 115. Try using it in your next meeting. Try using it on your own and see what thoughts it encourages.

give a little TLC

Is your company open and receptive to new ideas? What happens when someone comes up with an idea? What sort of reaction do new ideas get from the rest of the organisation? Often, ideas are greeted with things like, 'We tried that before' or 'It's too expensive'.

Being negative is one of the quickest ways to show a lack of commitment and to kill innovation even before it has started. Just be thankful you were not the person who came out with one of these negative reactions:

'But what is it good for?' Engineer at the Advanced Computing Systems Division of IBM, 1968, commenting on the microchip.

'There is no reason anyone would want a computer in their home.' Ken Olson, President, Chairman and founder of Digital Equipment Corp, 1977.

'This "telephone" has too many shortcomings to be seriously considered as a means of communication. The device is inherently of no value to us.' Western Union internal memo, 1876.

'The wireless music box has no imaginable commercial value. Who would pay for a message sent to nobody in particular?' David Sarnoff's associates in response to his urgings for investment in the radio in the 1920s.

'Who the hell wants to hear actors talk?' HM Warner, Warner Brothers, 1927.

'We don't like their sound, and guitar music is on the way out.' Decca Recording Co. rejecting the Beatles, 1962.

'Heavier-than-air flying machines are impossible.' Lord Kelvin, President, Royal Society, 1895.

'Drill for oil? You mean drill into the ground to try and find oil? You're crazy.' Drillers whom Edwin L Drake tried to enlist to his project to drill for oil in 1859.

'Airplanes are interesting toys but of no military value.' Marechal Ferdinand Foch, Professor of Strategy, Ecole Supérieure de Guerre.

'Everything that can be invented has been invented.' Charles H Duell, Commissioner, US Office of Patents, 1899.

'Louis Pasteur's theory of germs is ridiculous fiction.' Pierre Pachet, Professor of Physiology at Toulouse, 1872.

'640K ought to be enough for anybody.' Bill Gates, 1981.

How can *you* avoid having egg on your face? How can you make sure you don't throw the baby out with the bathwater? How can you ensure you are supporting new ideas and giving them a chance to grow and develop? How can you make sure that everyone you work with is open and receptive to new and different ideas?

One way to do this is to think TLC – 'Tempting, Lacking, Changing'. Imagine someone comes to you with the idea of putting your organisation's catalogue on the Internet. Instead of saying something like, 'No, our customers don't use the Internet, and anyway who would do it and pay for it?', say something like, 'This sounds an interesting idea. Let's see what is tempting about it. There might be a few problems with it but we may be able to change a few things. Let's have a look and see.' That is, ask:

- What's tempting about this idea?
- What's lacking in this idea?
- What needs changing in this idea for it to work?

Encourage others to use TLC as well. When you hear someone about to say 'Yes, but...', stop them. Ask them to show a bit of TLC. Use TLC in meetings as the standard way of reacting to anything new. Not only does it stop negative comments but it is also a great way to encourage further discussion.

For example, if someone did come to you with the idea of putting your organisation's catalogue on the Internet, how would you respond?

TLC for an Internet catalogue

Step 1: Think tempting. Think about what is tempting about the idea. All ideas have something going for them. Putting your organisation's catalogue on the Internet would reduce the cost of printing. You could make changes quickly without waste. You could use colour.

Step 2: Think lacking. Think what is lacking about the idea. Few ideas are perfect when they're first thought of. Putting your organisation's catalogue on the Internet could be difficult to do. You don't have the expertise to create the web pages. You also don't know how many of your clients actually use the Internet.

Step 3: Think changing. Think about what can be changed about the idea to make it work. What can be altered, improved or done to make the idea even better? What if you found out which of your clients use the Internet? Do any new or potential clients use the Internet? There might be a whole new market out there! The costs saved by not printing might more than offset buying the expertise to create the Web

pages. Suddenly the idea of putting your company's catalogue on the Internet does not seem so wild after all. A little
bit of TLC can give an idea a chance.

We used TLC in our own office when we introduced a new
product. We not only involved some of our customers in testing
the product but we gave them the TLC structure to follow. Not
only did they tell us what was wrong with the product, they
also gave us all the ideas to improve it. It is now a great success.

tools of the trade
*Refer to Activity 7, TLC, on page 117. Try completing it with
an idea in mind. It could be the beginning of a major breakthrough!*

We have now tried four techniques that show your commitment – Creating thinking space, the Ladder, 'What if...?' and
TLC. Use some or all of these techniques and you have done
the important thing. You will have 'led the charge'. You will
have been one of the first people to be innovative. You will
have tried a few things, got a few new ideas and encouraged
others to do the same. You will have shown your commitment.

Now is the time to encourage others to follow your lead, to
join in the charge and be more innovative. It is time to become
an actively innovative leader.

the three As of innovative leadership

Leadership must be one of the most written-about topics of
today. Everyone has his or her own thoughts, theories and
ideas as to what type or style of leadership we need in order to
face the future positively. While everyone seems to have his or
her own unique approach to leadership, there seems to be a
common thread to what everyone is saying. Leadership is
about getting people to follow you, willingly.

Innovation requires that people follow you willingly. Innovations come from people who willingly contribute and develop their ideas. The three As of innovative leadership (see Figure 3.2) will help you achieve willing followers, people committed to innovation.

Alighting	employees with a sense of their own purpose
Aligning	employees to the organisational purpose
Allowing	employees the freedom to challenge and change the way they work

Figure 3.2 *The three As of innovative leadership*

The three As of innovative leadership do not work in isolation. They tend to happen all at the same time, one feeding into the other forming a never-ending cycle of activity.

Having said *alighting*, *aligning* and *allowing* all work together, let's look at each one in turn, to understand what each involves. Then we can look at them as a whole and see how they feed one into the other and work together.

alighting

How many times have you heard a child say 'I didn't do it on purpose'? How many times have *you* said it? Maybe sometimes it is better to deny responsibility. Sometimes it is better for things to have been accidental. This is not the case with innovation. With innovation, you want people to say the exact opposite. You want people to say 'I did it on purpose!'

The world has been full of people who have 'done it on purpose'. The Wright brothers flew... after 805 attempts. The Wright brothers flew 'on purpose'. Michelangelo took many years to complete the Sistine Chapel, that is, he painted 'on purpose'. Most innovations occur on purpose. Even when they occur 'by accident', it is because someone was looking for *something.* Innovation occurs because people want it to. It occurs because people put their effort into something.

If you want innovation, then you need people to do it 'on purpose'.

getting people to do it 'on purpose'

To develop a sense of purpose throughout the organisation that encourages innovation, you need to deal with organisational purpose, individual purpose (both yours and others') and team purpose.

You can ensure that your people are 'alight' with purpose in a formal or informal way. The informal way simply means you talk purpose at every opportunity. Whenever you talk about the organisation, talk about its purpose. Start meetings reminding people of the purpose and how important it is. When talking to individuals, focus on individual purpose. The more you talk about the idea of purpose and share it, the more others will understand it and use it.

The other way to 'alight' people is more formal. This formal process is a number of steps designed to get everyone consciously thinking about and working towards developing a clear sense of purpose. It takes a bit longer but it is great if you can achieve it.

Step 1: Define organisational purpose. Be clear about the organisation's purpose and the part innovation plays in it. We covered how to develop organisational purpose at the beginning of this chapter. If you complete the Organisational Purpose Worksheet on page 112 in Chapter 5, you will have this clearly in mind. If you have not done this yet, complete it before you move forward.

Once you have a clear organisational purpose in mind, you can move forward to the next step.

tools of the trade

Refer to Activity 4, Organisational Purpose, on pages 110–11.

Step 2: Your individual purpose. The next step is to clarify your purpose. What is it that turns you on? What is it that you really want to achieve? What is your individual purpose? This is important for two reasons. First, you need purpose to be an innovator yourself. Secondly, if you are going to help others clarify their purpose, you need to have worked through the process yourself.

The five 'Why's is a great exercise to help find out what turns you on and why. To get the five 'Why's to work for you, start by asking yourself why you do what you do.

Michael Morgan's five 'why's

When I asked myself the five 'Why's, the first question I asked was: 'Why do I run my own business?'. (Why No 1.) The answer was because I like the freedom, I like the variety and I like making my own decisions.

To determine the second Why question, simply turn your first answer into a question and ask yourself why that is important. In my example, Why No 2 became: 'Why do I like freedom, variety and making my own decisions?'. The answer was because I can then work on things I enjoy and like.

Why No 3 becomes: 'Why is it important to work on things I enjoy and like?'. The answer was that it is where I get my satisfaction. I get satisfaction out of discovering things, of doing new things, of learning new things.

Why No 4 is then: 'Why is it important to discover new things and to learn new things?'. Because, to me, that is what life is about. Life is about newness, about creativity, about discovery. Give me a job that allows me to do that and I will work 24 hours at it. That is what turns me on.

In this case, four 'Why's was enough to give me the clarity I needed. For me, life is about newness, creativity and discovery.

I was lucky. My individual purpose was all about newness, creativity and discovery. My organisational purpose was all about creating better business through better thinking. A perfect match.

You are now clear about organisational purpose and your individual purpose. It's now time to help others clarify their individual purpose.

tools of the trade
Refer to Activity 9, Alighting Individual Purpose, on page 121.

Step 3: Individual purpose for others. Many people will already know their own purpose and be working towards achieving it. Others may need help in clarifying what theirs is.

The best way to do this is to build it into a workshop or meeting format and make it part of your overall innovation strategy. Introduce the concept of purpose and explain how important it is to innovation. Give people a copy of the Alighting Individual Purpose Worksheet. Show them how you used it to develop *your* purpose. Share both the organisation's purpose and your purpose with them. Then allow them time to have a go at defining a purpose of their own. The objective here is not necessarily to have every individual in the organisation develop a clear purpose statement. That would be nice if you can achieve it, but the exercise is more about getting them to think about it, to think about the organisation's purpose and begin to think about how they can contribute.

innovation conference

One company I worked with started with what they called the 'Innovation Conference'. They organised a two-day workshop for everyone in the organisation – about 80 people. The morning of Day 1 was all about the organisation, where it was going, why innovation was important and what the organisation's purpose was. The rest of Day 1 and part of Day 2 was spent helping individuals develop and clarify their purpose. They were asked what was it that they wanted to get out of the organisation and how could they do it. They used the Alighting Individual Purpose to do this.

tools of the trade
Refer to Worksheet 9b, Helping Others Find Purpose, on page 123.

Step 4: Team purpose. Chapter 2 started talking about boats and how important it is that everyone knows which way they are headed. Whenever you get a team together, it's vital they know which direction they are headed and why. This is the team purpose.

One company I know formed a number of 'Innovation teams'. Each team was to work on an innovation project over a six-month period. To get the whole thing going, they ran a two-day Kick-off Conference. Day 1 was all about innovation and the organisation. On Day 2, the project teams worked together, getting to know each other, defining their team purpose and deciding on projects. The first projects were so successful they are now into the third round of innovation projects.

tools of the trade
Refer to Activity 10, Alighting Team Purpose, on page 124.

Alighting is an ongoing process. As people come and go from the organisation or from teams, it is important to continually remind everyone what it is you are trying to do and why. Once people have this sense of purpose, you can begin to explore what they have in common and how they can work together. This is the next step – aligning.

aligning

If your staff are now 'alight' with purpose, you have an organisation full of purpose – as everyone has the *same* purpose. Actually, that is unlikely. It is more likely that everyone will have their own purpose, their own force pulling them forward. The dilemma is obvious. You want people motivated, but not if it means they are heading off in their own direction.

If you are self-employed, then there is probably a perfect match between your purpose and your organisation's purpose. They are one and the same. But not all of us work for ourselves. Some of us work for large organisations where the organisation itself has a purpose and so does everyone else in it. The potential for chaos is great. This is where alignment comes in. It is vital to get everyone in the boat rowing in the same direction.

Alignment is the simple process of exploring individual and organisational purpose, finding out what they have in common and then working towards achieving both at the same time. You do this by continually talking to people about the organisation's purpose, asking them about their purpose and discussing how the two can work together.

Step 1: Tell everyone the organisation's purpose. Everyone needs to know where the organisation is headed. You need to openly discuss what the organisation is trying to do, what its goals and objectives are and why it is heading in that direction. The more that people know about the organisation, the easier it is for them to 'align' with it.

There are many ways to make sure everyone knows where the organisation is headed. Some companies hang posters on the walls and notice boards. Others send out regular newsletters and special publications. Others talk about it at every opportunity and every company function.

One company I know produced a 10-page booklet on innovation and the impact it would have on the organisation and everyone in it. It was very well received. Another company ran a series of information sessions. Everyone was invited to attend and everyone was encouraged to ask whatever they wanted. The open and honest answers people got went a long way to increasing everyone's commitment to innovation.

The secret to helping people understand where the organisation is headed is to express it in simple terms. As we saw earlier, you need to make sure the message is simple, memorable, magic and for everyone.

Step 2: Help people develop a sense of individual purpose. People who know what they are about and what they are trying to achieve are much more likely to focus on something, think about it and have innovative ideas about it. In his book, *Creating* (1994, Butterworth-Heinemann, Oxford), Robert Fritz says that a sense of individual purpose is the driving force that all creative people have in common. It is the one thing that separates them from the less creative. We discussed ways of helping people develop a sense of purpose when we talked about alighting.

Step 3: Combine organisational and individual purposes. Have you ever tried to walk beside someone, and stay there, as you make your way through a crowd? It's almost impossible without weaving and ducking and continually making adjustments in your stride, pace and direction. Sometimes you are side by side, and other times you are briefly separated as someone else comes between you. You have to continually work at staying together and not becoming separated.

This is what 'aligning' is all about. Aligning is the process of getting and keeping two things heading in the same direction at roughly the same pace. In this case it is an individual and the organisation – you want to get them heading in roughly the same direction for as long as you can. Aligning is also something you have to keep doing. It is not something that you do once and then forget all about.

Chris was the CEO of a retail company. He stood in his

office one day and said, 'My job is to have the biggest impact I can on this company. I cannot do it by sitting in this office.' So he spent most of his time out of the office talking to people and working directly with his staff. He was highly effective and everyone knew exactly why they were there and the contribution they made.

Because aligning is an ongoing process, there is no one way to achieve it. It involves doing many things over time. Take every opportunity to talk about it. These opportunities will be both formal and informal. The formal opportunities include such things as an induction discussion, annual career discussions, regular performance reviews and any other scheduled management discussion you have with someone. The informal opportunities include allocating new tasks, reviewing progress and any general discussions you have.

As well as aligning individuals, a team can also benefit from being aligned, whenever it meets. It should certainly be a big part of any initial team discussion about why the team exists in the first place. It can then form the basis of any discussion that the team has whenever it meets.

tools of the trade
Refer to Activity 11, The Aligning Process, on page 126. It will help you work through the aligning process.

allowing
Imagine trying to muster a herd of cattle on your own. With almost every beast in the herd charging off in different directions, you will probably need horses, helpers, highly-skilled cattle dogs, possibly even helicopters to get them to do anything you want.

The cattle round up is a bit like managing a non-aligned organisation. With no common purpose, everyone will be charging off in different directions. To get anyone to do anything, you need to introduce some pretty effective controls. These controls vary from a highly specific task manual, to watertight job descriptions, to inspectors at every stage of the process and penalties for under-performance. The entire management structure would need to be designed around control.

If you have alignment (if you have everyone headed in the same direction), then something very profound happens. To start with, you certainly don't need all the horses, helicopters, helpers and dogs. All you need is the pull of that common purpose. You can shift from 'managing by control' to 'leading by allowing'.

Innovation requires free thinking. It requires people to think outside the box, to think differently. If you want people to think in this way then you need to give them the freedom to do so. You need to give them the freedom to explore, question, experiment, rearrange, modify and think for themselves. You need to give them the freedom to challenge and change the way they work. If you confine someone, tie them down and force them to stick to particular thought patterns, you leave little or no room for this freedom of thought.

Think of those people who are creative, with or without you. In many cases, the more you try to confine them, the more they ignore you. They do not respond to your bureaucratic procedures. They shun your schedules. They will resist most of your attempts to make them efficient. They are not doing this out of malice. They are simply working to their agenda, not yours. They are free. These naturally creative people need freedom. Other people may need encouragement to take it.

Encouraging innovation has always been like walking a tightrope between anarchy and oppression. On the one hand, you want people challenging everything you do. On the other, you need conformity to certain procedures. You need a balance between individual choice and organisational control.

giving people their freedom

You now face the freedom challenge. It is a challenge made easier by the fact that most people accept that the organisation has the right to decide *what* has to be done. All you have to do is give them freedom in *how* to do it.

Small is beautiful. One way is to stay small. The smaller the business unit, the fewer controls are needed, the more communication there is between people and the more closely they can work together. Some organisations actually structure themselves around small business units rather than operating as one large organisation. Small means less administration and more personal freedom. Being small can tilt the balance towards personal choice.

Freedom of choice. Some occupations have specific uniforms. Pilots, chefs, police officers and the armed forces all have official uniforms. Some occupations have informal ones, like suits for bankers and accountants, and overalls for mechanics and painters.

On the other hand, some companies have no strict dress codes. Some companies allow research workers to work the hours that suit them and have offices that are somewhat unusual. There are quite a few companies now that have 'casual dress days'. Usually on a Friday, you can wear what you like. Other companies have casual dress as part of meetings and workshops. How much personal freedom of choice is there in your organisation?

Crossing barriers. Most of us have never questioned the right to travel. If we want to go somewhere, we just get in our cars or on a plane and go. We are free to explore new places and meet new people, and in doing so we learn new things. We learn how other people think and how they live. Travel is one of the great gifts of the modern world. But it is a gift that not everyone in this world shares. In some countries people are not allowed to travel more than a few kilometres. Travel means knowledge and knowledge means challenge, change and creativity – the creativity that comes from freedom.

If you want innovation, you need to encourage people to travel as much as they can. Form work groups made up of people from many different parts, let them join groups from other sections, visit other parts of the organisation to see how they operate, rotate jobs, second people and welcome visitors.

I use the Internet to cross barriers and travel. I have four discussion groups operating at the moment. They all have between three and six people in them and all the people live in different countries. It is a quick, easy and effective way to exchange ideas and cross any number of barriers.

What, not how. When mustering, once you have all the cattle going in the same direction, the less you do, the better. As long as they are all headed in the same general direction, leave them to it. You may need to guide the occasional stray but most will manage themselves and choose their own way through the fields. People are the same. Once you have alignment – that is, they are all headed in roughly the same direction – let them choose their own way. Tell people what you want done but give them the freedom to choose how they do it. If you tell them what to do and how to do it, you reduce the amount of personal freedom. In some jobs, that is essential, in others less so.

John, a national sales manager, was a great example of the 'what, not how' approach to management. John had about 45 sales people in his team. They were known as the most innovative in the industry in the way they did things. John would get them together each year for their annual sales conference. The objective of the sales conference was to explain the 'what' for the next 12 months. He wanted to make sure everyone knew and was committed to the same objectives. He also then stressed that his role was to provide whatever help and support they needed to achieve the objectives. How they achieved their individual goals was up to them, so long as they did it in an ethical manner and within the guidelines he laid down.

Each month they would have a sales meeting. They would review their sales for the month and then brainstorm ideas for achieving them the next month. Everyone was involved in the meetings and everyone came up with ideas. John did not have to tell them how to do things. They came up with their own ideas on how to do the job – ideas that were always new and innovative and contributed to the high level of sales the team achieved.

Tolerate mistakes. No one wants to fail. No one wants to be the person who didn't make it to the top of the mountain, who didn't finish a race, who failed a final exam. There is not much future in being part of an organisation that fails either. We all want to succeed in one way or another. We are taught almost every day that success is what the world is all about.

In our drive for success, we often forget the important part that mistakes play in our lives. Over 90 per cent of what we do in our lives involves making some sort of mistake. Children learn through mistakes. Nearly everything they do fails the first time. They drop their bottle, they spill their food, they fall over, they fall off and they fall down. It is only through repeated mistakes and trying again that they succeed.

It is through not accepting failure that they succeed. Few children are able to walk the first time. They struggle and try again, the proud parents encouraging them at every bump until eventually the child totters around the room. Success. If we punished children every time they tried something and failed, they would not learn very much. The child would probably never walk.

Creativity is exactly the same. The quickest and surest way to kill creativity is to punish it when it does not work. The history of flight, for example, is full of magnificent failures that only served to drive people harder to find the secret. Remember, it took the Wright brothers over 805 attempts to get it right. Even then they only flew a matter of metres.

You should now be beginning to juggle both purpose and commitment. You have developed a sense of purpose in the organisation. The organisation has a clear sense of where it is headed and why. Remember, it is something that is simple, memorable, magic and for everyone. You have also started to show your commitment to innovation. You have begun to make changes, to act differently and to support others as they do the same. You are becoming an innovative leader. People should now be beginning to think for themselves more, showing more initiative and coming up with more and more ideas.

juggling ideas

It is now time to develop some skills in how to be an innovative thinker, in how to take those steps and jumps that are so important to innovation. It is now time to start juggling with ideas.

the Grand Canyon

Have you ever been to the Grand Canyon? From the top of it, you look down over this huge deep chasm with the Colorado River, looking like just a trickle, meandering through the bottom. Fly over it and you get a greater appreciation of how big it really is. From the foot of the canyon it is even more awe-inspiring. The cliffs tower above you and the white water of the river thunders past. The rocks, the colours and the sheer size of it can take your breath away. The Grand Canyon is one of the natural wonders of the world.

Do you know how the Grand Canyon was formed? What made it the way it is? The answer is erosion. The Colorado River has slowly eroded the earth away, cutting ever deeper into the earth, creating the canyon we see today. Each time it rained, the river would flow a little faster. Each time the snow from the mountains melted, it would roar across the rocks. Each time this happened, it would follow the same path. Each time it would cut a little deeper. The Colorado River, magnificent though it is, has no other way to flow but through the canyon. It has no other way to flow but the way it did last time, and the time before, the time before that....

mental erosion

Our minds are a bit like the Grand Canyon. Our minds are big, deep and awe-inspiring. Our minds are one of the natural wonders of the world. And like the Grand Canyon, they suffer from erosion – mental erosion.

Instead of water flowing through our minds, we have thoughts. Something happens to us and thoughts flow through us. When the same thing happens again, the same thoughts come flooding back, again and again. Each time we repeat what we did the last time, we cut that mental pathway a little deeper into our minds, causing mental erosion.

This is not all bad. If we had to stop and think about everything we did as if it was for the first time, we would get nowhere. Mental pathways and a bit of erosion are good in some circumstances. They are great for getting through the day, getting us to work and for times when we really don't need to think too much about something. But they can get in the way when we want to do something differently, when we want to break out and move in a different direction. Then it becomes hard. It is impossible for the Colorado River to flow a different way. Sometimes it seems impossible for us to think a different way.

thinking about innovation

Imagine for a moment that you work for the XYZ company. You have an idea about how to reduce delivery time. You think you have come up with a new way of sorting orders and getting them out of the warehouse faster. What do you do?

You talk to a few colleagues about it. You sound them out, see what they think. They seem to like the idea and suggest you take it further. You go to your managers and explain it. They have a few ideas of their own to add and they help you write a brief description of it. You enter it into XYZ's Suggestion Scheme.

Word comes back that 'they' like it. You are asked to make a presentation to the innovation committee. You prepare and give your presentation. The decision is made to test your idea. You are made part of a small project team. During the next months you test it, fiddle with it, argue over it, change it a bit and fight for it. Finally, some nine months after you first had this idea, something close to it is implemented within the warehouse.

Three months later, you have to say a few words as you collect the annual Innovation Award for the brightest idea of the year.

Innovation is a lot more than just having an idea. Innovation is about having ideas, talking to others about them, selling them to other people, describing them, testing them, fighting for them, improving them and implementing them.

Innovation requires that people get out of their Grand Canyon and head off in new and different directions. Innovation requires that people have lots of ideas and do things with them. This is where The IDEA Process can help.

The IDEA Process

The IDEA Process (© Michael Morgan 2000) helps people get out of whatever mental canyon they are in by thinking in new and different ways. It helps people think through the entire innovation process. It helps them anticipate things, define things, solve things, create things and implement things.

The IDEA Process is built around the acronym IDEA:

■ *Initiating*. It means anticipating the future, being one step ahead of the market, solving small problems before they become big ones, creating new opportunities, out-thinking the competition, designing innovative products, being ahead of the game, being first, setting the pace, creating the future.

▓ *Defining.* It means dealing with the right issue at the right level, having many points of view, having lots of problems to work on, being spot on, dealing with the cause, setting yourself up for creative solutions, having many different descriptions of problems, seeing problems positively.

▓ *Exploring.* It means having lots of ideas, solutions and perspectives, listening to intuition and insight, building ideas on ideas, selecting interesting ideas, keeping your thoughts together, brainstorming, daydreaming and think tanks.

▓ *Acting.* It means keeping the energy going, overcoming barriers, gaining commitment, implementing ideas, taking innovation to market, managing the idea to completion, making it happen.

The IDEA Process helps people think in new and different ways. It consists of a number of techniques that help people to think outside the square. It helps people to think through the entire innovation process.

initiating The IDEA Process

Initiating is anticipating the future, being one step ahead of the market, solving small problems before they become big ones, creating new opportunities, out-thinking the competition, designing innovative products, being ahead of the game, being first, setting the pace, creating the future.

Have you ever ridden in a car when the driver is driving on the brake lights of the car in front? What sort of ride do you get? It is usually highly stressful as your driver reacts immediately to what is happening. Everything happens at a furious pace. It is a stop-start affair, with no time to anticipate anything. And the chance of ending up in the back of the car in front is very high.

Imagine, on the other hand, driving with someone who drives on the brake lights of the car 10 cars in front. They watch everything up ahead, they anticipate, they have time to slow down, speed up and change lanes. Everything happens at a much more relaxed pace. You have time to anticipate what is coming up and enjoy what is going on.

Many organisations today are driving on the brake lights of the car in front. They are reacting, not anticipating. They are rushing around with hardly time to do anything else but concentrate on what is just ahead. Life, for some organisations and for the people in them, is highly stressful. This is not the best way to innovate.

Imagine working for an organisation that anticipates what is happening, that always seems to have time to do things and get things done. Imagine an organisation that is ahead of the game and has an eye to the future. This is the sort of organisation where innovation can flourish.

This is what the *initiating* is all about. It means changing your focus from the short term to the long term. It is how to anticipate, and in some cases actually influence, the future. Initiating is the first step towards having ideas.

how to initiate
Let's take a look at some useful strategies in 'initiating'.

initiating 1: 'what if...?'
We discussed 'What if...?' earlier. It's a great way to show your commitment to innovation. It is a powerful technique to use in anticipating the future.

scenario planning at Shell

One of the best-known examples of 'What if...?', or scenario planning, occurred at Shell during the early 1970s. Shell was the first petroleum company to envisage the formation of OPEC and the sudden oil price shock that hit the world in 1973. In 1984, they also foresaw the possible break up of the Soviet Union and the ensuing chaos in Eastern Europe. In each case they were able to turn it into some sort of competitive advantage.

Try using 'What if...?' with your organisation. Begin by asking the sort of questions that no one usually asks. Begin by asking about things that are sacred, that are never questioned, that are taken for granted, that your business is built on.

For example, if you work in the finance industry, ask, 'What if there was no money?' In the computer industry, ask, 'What if computers caused cancer?' In the tourist industry, ask, 'What if our climate suddenly changed?' And in the food industry, ask, 'What if meat was found to be bad for people?'

Just think for a minute about the industry you are in. Ask yourself a few 'What if...?' questions about some of the things that are sacred, that are never questioned and that are taken for granted. What would happen if they changed in some way?

tools of the trade
Refer to Activity 12, 'What if...?', on page 127. Try completing it with your organisation in mind. Find out what it might tell you about the future.

I worked recently with a company trying to create a new future for itself. The MD, Alan, explained that they were currently number three in their industry. He wanted to be number one, but knew he could not do it by doing what everyone else was doing. So we used 'What if...?' to anticipate the future, to explore what might happen. In less than one hour, Alan's company had more new ideas than they had had in the previous six months.

'What if...?' is a simple technique that can shift your focus away from the brake lights of the car in front and help you anticipate what might happen in the future. You can use 'What if...?' to anticipate problems, to invent new products, to improve sales, to second-guess the competition and reposition an entire organisation. Innovative people are forward thinkers. Using 'What if...?' is one way they do it.

initiating 2: long jumping

Carl Lewis is probably the greatest of all Olympic athletes and certainly one of the best long jumpers the world has ever seen. I wonder how far Carl could jump from a standing start? Like Carl, when we jump, we want to jump as far as we can. And like Carl, we need to take a couple of steps backwards to do that. In the long jump, the 'run-up' is all important.

It's hard to jump into the future from a standing start. The long jump is a technique that helps you think about the future by getting you to jump mentally from the past to the future. It is like taking a few steps backwards – and then jumping as far as you can into the future.

long jumping a menu for 2020

Imagine you wanted to know what food might be like in the year 2020. Remember, no standing starts allowed. Take a couple of mental steps backwards and ask yourself:

Question: I wonder what the food was like in 400BC?
Answer: Probably not gourmet! More like an open fire and a rabbit on a stick.
Question: I wonder what the food was like in AD900?
Answer: Lamb, goat's milk, bread, wine and limited table manners.
Question: I wonder what the food was like in 1920?
Answer: Meat and two vegetables, not very adventurous, functional.

Question: What is food like now?
Answer: Gourmet, takeaway, low fat, high fat, lots of variety, multicultural.
Question: What will the food be like in 2020?
Answer: Based on rice, mainly vegetarian, fast and easy to prepare, artificially flavoured.

If you work in the food industry, that gives you a lot of food for thought! You can now use your ideas to drive innovation and anticipate the future.

So how do you long jump? There are five simple steps:

1. Pick something to wonder about and a time frame to do it in. For example, 'I wonder what food will be like in the year 2020'?
2. Take three steps backwards. Pick three times in history to go back to. Try and spread them out so you get a good feeling of change and time. For example, try using 400BC, AD900, 1920 and today.
3. Wonder. For each historical period, wonder what it would have been like.
4. Jump. Wonder what it will be like in the future time you picked. Have fun, dream, play with some ideas, be silly. Just write down any thoughts that come to mind.
5. Wonder about *your* future. If you are to succeed in the future you have described, what will you have to look like? What will you need to do? How will you need to be different? It is the answer to this question that will drive innovation for you.

tools of the trade
Refer to Activity 13, Long Jumping, on page 129. Try completing it with your organisation in mind. Find out what it might tell you about the future.

I used long jumping with Alan and his top team. Alan was CEO of a company that imported and distributed a range of floor coverings. The business was ranked third in the industry. Alan wanted it to be number one. He knew that he could not achieve that by doing the same as everyone else. He knew that the business had to do things differently. The challenge was to work out exactly what things needed to be different and in what way. Alan wanted to create a new and exciting future for the business that would leap-frog it over the others. He did this by using long jumping as the way to plan the future.

Long jumping allowed him to create a number of different future scenarios. He was then able to pick the most likely three and develop them further. He then selected the one that would give him the best chance of achieving his goal of being number one.

When speaking to Alan recently, he said they were ahead of their plans and were excited about the possibilities. He felt confident that they had come up with the right strategy and were well on the way to achieving their goal.

Long jumping is a great technique to get people thinking about the future. It is especially good for dealing with more complex questions such as where an organisation should be heading, anticipating industry trends and market needs.

Initiating is the first stage of The IDEA Process. It is about anticipating the future, being one step ahead of the market, solving small problems before they become big ones, creating new opportunities, out-thinking the competition, designing innovative products, being ahead of the game, being first, setting the pace, creating the future.

The two techniques, 'What if…?' and long jumping, help you anticipate things. They help you come up with lots of ideas about what might happen and what you could make happen. They shift your focus away from the brake lights of the car in front to the brake lights way up ahead. They shift your focus away from the problems of today to the challenges of tomorrow.

By shifting your focus away from today and onto tomorrow, they also give you time to think. They make you proactive instead of reactive. And innovation is all about being proactive. It takes time to innovate. It takes time to come up with an idea, to think it through, develop it, test it and implement it. And the only way to have that time is to be thinking about the future, to be anticipating, to be second-guessing, to be initiating.

defining The IDEA Process

Dealing with the right issue at the right level, having many points of view, having lots of problems to work on, being spot on, dealing with the cause, setting yourself up for creative solutions, having many yet different descriptions of problems, seeing problems positively.

You cannot anticipate everything. You cannot drive solely on the brake lights up ahead. Sometimes you do have to react to the car in front. Sometimes you do have to react quickly, with little time and no anticipation. When this happens, the urge to fix it quickly and act now is overpowering. When this happens, it is hard to be innovative. It is this sort of situation that led Einstein to say: 'If the world was going to end in 60 minutes, I would spend the first 55 minutes working out what the problem was and 5 minutes fixing it.' If that sort of thinking worked for Einstein, perhaps it can work for us.

Initiating and anticipating things is one opportunity for innovation. Problem solving and reacting to things is another. This is when 'defining the issue' becomes important. Defining is making sure you are dealing with the right issue in the right way. You may not be able to stop for 55 minutes as Einstein suggested, but you can take 5 to make sure you are dealing with the right thing in the right way.

define the problem right for success

There are many examples of people defining problems incorrectly and fixing the wrong thing. I did it the other day with the gutters on our house. In heavy rain, water poured out where the gutters joined each other. Filling the gaps would obviously fix the problem! So I filled the gaps and the next time it rained the water still poured out. The problem turned out to be the slope of the gutters. They sloped away from the down pipes. The water had nowhere to go so found its way out through the gaps. Fixing the slope of the gutters and encouraging the water to flow to the down pipes solved the problem.

Another example of the need for more than one definition of an issue was with our annual client conference. People were slow in registering. Our immediate reaction was to send out a reminder with a special 'early-bird' offer. When we did this it got the same poor response as before. It turned out the issue was something else entirely. The reason why people were slow in responding was that I had sent the material out as an attachment to an e-mail. There were lots of people who were unable to download the attachment and read it. So one click and it got lost. As soon as we discovered this and changed the format, registrations poured in.

how to define the issue

Defining is also about having lots of definitions of the problem. You need to be as creative in defining the problem as you do solving it. Innovation feeds off problems, challenges, opportunities and concerns.

Defining is important for two reasons. It makes sure you are dealing with the right issue and makes sure there are lots of them to deal with! Here we look at ways to define the issue constructively.

defining 1: Who Do What

Imagine for a moment you are in charge of sales for a toy manufacturer. You decide you want to increase sales by 10 per cent. What would you do? Why not call a sales meeting, discuss the issue and brainstorm ideas about how to increase sales? This is probably how most people would go about it.

Another way is to use a technique like 'Who do what' and come up with as many different definitions about the issue as you can *before* you start brainstorming ideas. And then, when you do start brainstorming, brainstorm about three or four issues, not just one. This way you are much more likely to come up with some innovative ideas and get your 10 per cent increase in sales.

Let's look at an example. You want to increase sales by 10 per cent. Start by defining the issue as: 'How can we increase sales by 10 per cent?'. Then write 'Who', 'Do', and 'What' across a page, as headings for three columns. Under 'Who', write 'we'; under 'Do', write 'increase'; under 'What', write 'sales up by 10 per cent'.

Now it's time for some brainstorming. But this is brainstorming about problems rather than ideas. Under the heading 'Who', list 10 other 'Whos' you can think of – customers, suppliers, teenagers, parents, males, computers, machines, pensioners, accountants, the government – anyone you can think of. Move to the next column, the 'Do' column, and repeat the process. You might list decrease, speed up, slow down, improve, expand, communicate, enthuse, negotiate, motivate and stop. Finally, do the same for the 'What' column, listing 10 'Whats'. The end result could look like Figure 3.3.

Instead of the one original definition of how to increase sales by 10 per cent, you have 10 new questions to consider. As a friend of mine always says, 'Innovation starts with having more problems than you know what to do with.'

The next step is where the fun starts. You pick one word from each column and write it down as a problem statement. Then you start to brainstorm ideas about how to address the

	Who	Do	What
	How can we	increase	sales by 10%
1.	customers	decrease	profit
2.	suppliers	speed up	delivery
3.	teenagers	slow down	competition
4.	parents	improve	customers
5.	males	expand	costs
6.	computers	communicate	image
7.	machines	enthuse	stock
8.	pensioners	negotiate	product appeal
9.	accountants	motivate	new products
10.	government	stop	performance

Figure 3.3   *Who Do What*

problem. For example, if we selected the fourth, sixth and third words, we would get 'parents', 'communicate' and 'competition'. Make it into a problem statement such as, 'How can parents communicate with or about the competition?' Now have a brainstorming session on the statement and see what ideas you get. When I used this method, I immediately thought about parents and the concerns that they have with toys. These concerns are often about safety, price and durability. If we could convince parents that our toys were the safest, it could boost sales. What about getting parents to give us feedback, not about *our* toys but about the competition's toys? We would then know more about what they liked and didn't like.

Carry on brainstorming ideas until you start to run out of ideas. As soon as that happens, go back to the list and choose another combination of three words. For example, my second pick is the numbers five, nine and two, which give me 'males', 'motivate' and 'delivery'. This gives me the statement, 'How can males motivate delivery?' Brainstorming this, I came up with the idea of iron men selling toys in shops, a home delivery toy service, a special toy range for boys and a new range of executive toys for adults.

When you have exhausted the list of definitions and have a room full of ideas, go back to your original statement: 'How can we increase sales by 10 per cent?' Look through your list of ideas and see which ones have potential. The chances are that you have a lot more to choose from than if you had stayed with the original single narrow definition. And who knows, you could end up with a 20 per cent increase.

tools of the trade
Refer to Activity 14, Who Do What, on page 131. Try completing it with an issue of your own in mind.

defining 2: the ladder
We have already used the ladder as a way of showing commitment; look again at Figure 3.1. It is not only a great way to show your commitment but also a great way to make sure you are dealing with an issue at the right level. Earlier we used the example of 'making your organisation more innovative' (see Figure 3.1); it can also help us deal with 'increasing our sales by 10 per cent'.

Draw your ladder and write, 'How can we increase sales by 10 per cent?' on a central rung. Now go up a rung and write down a broader definition. For example, going up the ladder might be:

- ▨ How can we make the entire organisation more profitable?
- ▨ How can the entire organisation increase sales by 10 per cent?
- ▨ How can we increase sales in all products by 10 per cent?

Going down the ladder might be:

- How can I increase my sales by 10 per cent?
- How can I increase my sales to a specific customer by 10 per cent?
- How can I increase sales of one specific product?

Innovation is as much about knowing at what level to work at as it is about coming up with lots of ideas. The ladder is a great way of finding the best level, or levels, to work on.

tools of the trade
Refer to Activity 15, The Ladder Workshop, on page 133. Try using it on a problem or issue you are facing and see if it gives you a different perspective on things.

too much on my mind!
You should now have more problems than you know what to do with. This is one of the secrets to innovation. The more problems you have, the more things you have to think about. The more things you have to think about, the more likely you are to come up with those great ideas. 'Who do what' and 'The ladder' are two techniques that can really help. 'Who do what' gives you lots of things to think about and 'The ladder' helps you deal with it at the most appropriate level or levels.

Now you know what the problem or issue is, it's time to come up with ideas about acting on it.

exploring The IDEA Process

Exploring is having lots of ideas, solutions and perspectives, listening to intuition and insight, building ideas on ideas, selecting interesting ideas, keeping your thoughts together, brainstorming, daydreaming and think tanks.

Have you noticed how some people never seem to be short of ideas? It is as if their heads are full of them, all just waiting to pop out. In most cases, their heads are *not* full of ideas, but they do have the ability to generate lots in a very short time. They do this by suspending judgement. Suspending judgement means not bothering about how good the idea is yet. There is plenty of time (and usually lots of willing people) to see just how good they are. Exploring is just getting on with coming up with as many ideas as possible. It's like turning the tap on and letting them flow. It is actually very easy to do with the right techniques.

exploring 1: brainstorming

'Brainstorming' is doing just that – it's cooking up a storm of ideas as quickly and efficiently as you can. It occurs best in groups, everyone yelling out their ideas as they get them. Quantity, not quality, is the order of the day. Evaluation of ideas does not occur till after the session finishes.

To get the best out of a brainstorming session, you need to set it up correctly. You need to have:

- ▩ a well-defined and clearly stated problem;
- ▩ someone assigned to write down all the ideas as they occur;
- ▩ the right number of people in the group;
- ▩ someone in charge;
- ▩ the rules of brainstorming.

a well-defined and clearly stated problem

With a group of people all yelling out ideas, you had better have a clear focus or it could end up anywhere. A good brain-storming session will have a very clear goal or objective, some-thing that everyone has clearly in mind all the time. While it is important that ideas flow freely and that people build one on the other, it must bring you back to where you want to be. The way to do this is to have a very clear goal or problem on which to work. Something like 'Improve overall customer service' is too broad. 'Reduce customer waiting time' is more specific and is likely to yield better ideas.

someone assigned to write down ideas as they occur

It's always a good idea to have specific roles assigned before you start. One of the most important roles is the writer, someone who will faithfully write down every idea, usually on a flipchart, for everyone to see. The ideas should be written down quickly and clearly so they stimulate other ideas. Make sure you have lots of paper and Blu-tack available, so that as you fill one piece of paper you can keep on going with the next. There is nothing worse in a brainstorming session than having to stop while you get more paper. It's like sprinting – when you keep stopping, it's very hard to get going again.

the right number of people in the group

If there are more than 10 to 12 people, then you will have chaos. You end up with too many people, with too many ideas, and it becomes impossible for everyone to contribute. Likewise, if there are less than about eight people, you don't have enough energy to keep it going. People will have a run of ideas for a few minutes, back off a little while they listen and think, and then join in again for another few minutes. Less than eight people and you don't have enough to allow for this ebb and flow.

someone in charge

You're all ready to go. You have a clear goal in mind, you have someone all ready to write down the ideas as they tumble out and you have 10 bright, energetic people ready to go. You still need the most important ingredient of a successful brainstorming session – someone to keep it on track and to keep it moving. This person needs to make sure everyone follows the basic rules of brainstorming.

the rules of brainstorming
There are four crucial rules of brainstorming:

■ judgement is suspended;
■ every idea is accepted and recorded;
■ people are encouraged to build on the ideas of others;
■ way-out and odd ideas are encouraged.

No criticism or comments on the quality of ideas are allowed. In brainstorming, you are after as many ideas as you can get. At this stage you are not concerned with how good they are or how way-out or odd they appear. You simply want ideas, nothing else. One of the quickest ways to kill off a brainstorming session is for someone to yell out an idea and for someone else to immediately say, 'Oh don't be silly, that will never work'.

Brainstorming is all about people withholding judgement on how good the ideas are till the end of the session. To withhold judgement is not as easy as it sounds as we are taught to judge almost everything all the time. You need someone who will stop any negative or judgmental comments before they get in the way of ideas.

Hopefully the session will be energetic, with ideas flying fast and furious. No one will be able to remember what was said five minutes ago. You need someone not only writing the ideas down, but also making sure every idea is written clearly and correctly. People get more ideas by looking at the written list. Ensure the writing is big and clear for all to see.

Not every idea needs to be new and unique. Some of the best ideas can come from building on or adding to an existing idea. You need to encourage people to do this. If the energy is dropping and the flow of ideas is slowing down a bit, refer back to the list. Pick any idea from the list and yell it out. Keep doing this. Keep going back over the list – asking questions, throwing old ideas out until someone comes up with a new thought and away you go again. It is important to keep the energy up and the ideas flowing.

Quantity of ideas is what you are after. Even in a well-managed brainstorming session people are sometimes reluctant to come up with way-out ideas – but you need these way-out ideas. So you need to encourage people to share them. The best way to do this is to make sure there are no negative comments flying around and to offer a few ideas yourself. Model what you want from the group.

Before athletes compete in a race, they usually warm up first. This gets the muscles warmed up and the blood pumping so that when the gun goes, they are off to a good start. Warming up can be an important part of brainstorming as well. Have a trial brainstorming session on a dummy topic first. This gets people ready, teaches them the rules and gets the energy going. Then when everyone is firing and the ideas are flowing, you can change to your real problem statement. A good 20 minutes is usually enough time to develop a full list of ideas. Only at the end, when everyone has run out of ideas and is as exhausted as if they had been in a race, can you type up the list of ideas, circulate it to those involved and begin to evaluate the ideas.

Brainstorming is harder than it sounds to do properly. The hardest thing is to resist judging. We judge other people's ideas and say things like, 'That's silly' or 'That will never work'. We also judge our own ideas as we think of them and don't offer them to the group. The leader needs to create an open climate and really encourage people to give their ideas.

tools of the trade
Refer to Worksheet 16, Brainstorming, on page 136. Try running a session and see how many ideas you can come up with in a short period of time.

exploring 2: mixing metaphors
Imagine you are trying to invent a new waterproof fabric. You need to decide what properties it should have. Suddenly a thought comes to mind: 'Like water off a duck's back'. You ask yourself: 'What would happen if water ran off the fabric like

water off a duck's back?'. Your mind races. 'Yes', you think, 'that will work'.

Duck's feathers have an oily feel about them that repels water. They are wonderfully soft, and when they get water on them, all the duck has to do is give them a shake and they are all fluffed up again. What about a fabric that does that?

'Like water off a duck's back' is an example of a metaphor. Using a metaphor is a great way to gain a fresh insight into something. Imagine for a moment that you are thinking about where to go for your next holiday. You are stuck for a good idea. Instead of reaching for the holiday brochures, why not take a fresh look at the chair you're sitting in! How is that chair like the holiday you want? The chair is soft to sit in. It does not move. It has a nice bright covering. You sit in it to eat. It was not too expensive. Now think of that holiday. A soft relaxing holiday where you don't have to move around, in the sunshine, with good food and wine that is not too expensive. Sounds perfect. Now look in the brochure and find somewhere that fits what you want.

Imagine you have been asked to say a few words at a friend's birthday party. Instead of being stuck for words, you can now grab the nearest chair and say: 'In many ways Tom reminds me of this chair. He has always been strong and reliable, always there when you needed him most. Yet Tom has his soft side as well, always being warm and approachable and a true friend...'.

Words will begin to flow in a way you never believed possible. By using a chair to help you, you will never be stuck for an idea again!

Metaphors work just as well for complicated issues. Imagine you are sitting at your desk thinking about how you can improve the internal communication system in your organisation. You glance out of the window and see a big tree in the park. 'That's the problem,' you say to yourself. 'I can't see the roots of the tree. I can't see the roots of our communication system.'

You begin to explore the tree in your mind. The top half of the tree you can see; your external communication systems you can see. The top half of the tree bends in the wind; the bottom half lies rigid in the ground. Suddenly you realise that here is your problem – inflexible internal systems that do not respond to what is happening around them.

Metaphors are one of the most powerful ways of coming up with ideas. Einstein dreamed he was riding on a beam of light and wondered what the world would look like from that perspective. He then went home to do the sums. If metaphors worked for Einstein, perhaps they will work for us.

how to think in metaphors

So, how do we put the idea of metaphors to work for us? Here's how, in six steps:

1. Have something in mind that you want ideas about.
2. Pick an object to use as a metaphor – a chair, table, tree.
3. List all the characteristics of the object.
4. Stop and think about each characteristic in turn. Do they give you any ideas? List down the ideas you get.
5. When you've run out of ideas, pick another object and start again. Keep going until you have lots of ideas.
6. Look at all your ideas and see what you have!

Let's take the question of how to make an organisation more innovative. Using the metaphor of a chair, I would ask the question, 'In what way is this organisation like a chair?' and then list all the characteristics I found in common.

Both are rigid, both are comfy, supportive, stationary, padded and heavy. What insights does that give me about my organisation? What ideas come to mind about how to make the organisation more innovative? We could support new ideas more. We could move people around from department to department. We could introduce a competition for the best idea. We could refuse to take things so seriously... and so on.

---

how is my organisation like a circus?

Sometimes I find using a chair a bit limiting. I run out of ideas too soon. When this happens I use something more rich and complex to compare it with. I use something like a zoo, a circus or a train. Now the ideas really start to flow. How is my organisation like a circus?

- ■ There are lots of clowns.
- ■ People wear funny clothes.
- ■ Everyone goes round in circles.
- ■ People laugh.
- ■ People eat and have fun.
- ■ It is full of animals.
- ■ The ringmaster makes sure it works the way it should.
- ■ People pay to see it.

Look through your list and see what comes to mind. What about an innovation champion, outside advisers, creative days, play days, involving families and customers, paying people for ideas...?

tools of the trade
Refer to Activity 17, Mixing Metaphors, on page 138. Try running a session and see if you can invent something new.

exploring 3: dicey ideas
Imagine you have to plan a fiftieth birthday party for a friend. What would you do? Where would you start? How could you make sure it was a truly memorable night?

Using 'dicey ideas', you could come up with over 200 ideas

in less than five minutes. And from 200 ideas there must surely be a few that would actually work!

Dicey ideas is a great way to randomly combine old thoughts into new ideas. It is a simple five-step process:

1. Break your task into as many separate aspects as possible.
2. From this list, pick the three that are the most important or significant.
3. Think of six alternatives for each one.
4. Arrange each of the three lists into columns.
5. Throw the dice. If you don't like that idea, throw again till you find one that you do.

fantastic 50th

For example, in planning a 50th birthday for your best friend, you should think about the venue, the theme, the food, a price range, timing, length, entertainment, guests and gifts. From this list, you pick three aspects: say, the venue, the theme and the food.

Next, we think of six alternatives for each of these aspects. The venue could be outdoors, in a restaurant, on a river cruise, on the beach, in the countryside, in an aeroplane. The theme could be the Roaring 40s, Movies, Pop Stars, Historical Figures, Bad Taste or The Next Life. The food could be bring-your-own, no food at all, finger food, a barbeque, Chinese, or you could cook it yourself. Now arrange these options in a grid:

	Venue	**Theme**	**Food**
1.	Outdoors	Roaring 40s	Bring-your own
2.	Restaurant	Movies	None
3.	River cruise	Pop stars	Finger food
4.	The beach	Historical figure	Barbeque
5.	The countryside	Bad taste	Chinese
6.	Aeroplane	The next life	Cook it yourself

Throw the dice and see what number you get. If you score a 4, count down the first column until you come to The beach – your venue. Throw the dice again. Scoring a 2 means Movies is your theme. Throw again and scoring a 5, count down the third column to Chinese. How about a beach party with everyone dressed up as a movie star and eating Chinese food?

Imagine you work in the marketing department in a finance company. You have to come up with some innovative ideas in the next five minutes. Using 'dicey ideas', you might end up with:

	Customers	Advertising	Products
1.	Teenagers	TV	Loans
2.	Couples	Radio	General insurance
3.	Animals	Direct	Life insurance
4.	Travellers	Inserts	Travel insurance
5.	The aged	Door-to-door	Health insurance
6.	Babies	The Olympics	Cars

Using the throw of a dice, find out how many unusual ideas you can come up with.

tools of the trade
Refer to Activity 18, Dicey Ideas, on page 140.

Brainstorming, metaphors and dicey ideas are three great techniques for exploring things and coming up with ideas. Using any one of these should give you more ideas than you know what to do with. And that is an important part of being innovative – having lots of ideas to work with.

acting The IDEA Process

This stage involves keeping the energy going, overcoming barriers, gaining commitment, implementing ideas, taking innovation to market, managing the idea to completion, making it happen.

Some of the world's best ideas are just that – ideas. They remain ideas and nothing ever happens to them. My head is full of ideas. The problem is that I get so excited about the *next* idea I rarely get round to doing anything about the one I thought of first.

Innovation is more than just having good ideas. Innovation is about implementing ideas and changing the way we do things. Innovation is solving problems, getting new ideas to market and finding better ways to work.

The 'A' of The IDEA Process – Acting – is all about implementation. It is all about taking action and turning ideas into reality. It is a four-step process that involves picking winners, improving the odds, seeing the finish line and making it happen. These translate into:

1. Selecting the ideas with the greatest potential.
2. Developing ideas further and modifying them as required.
3. Being very clear about the finished product and what it will look like.
4. Having a well-thought-through plan and turning your idea into reality.

picking a winner

You are spending a day at the races. You decide it would be a good idea to have a couple of bets. Where do you start? Which race do you bet on? Which horse do you pick? You could be like me and take a guess (probably losing), or you could apply a bit more method to your selection.

Innovation is very much like a day at the races. It is all about selecting ideas with the greatest potential. It's all about picking winners. In picking winning ideas, you can do what I do at the races and simply take a guess, or you can ask yourself two key questions about each idea. The two questions are: 1) What does this idea have working for it? 2) What does this idea have working against it?

Here's how you apply the questions. Imagine someone comes to you with an idea on how to speed up delivery and reduce costs at the same time. Their idea is to have all domestic deliveries ready to go by 4 pm, so deliveries can go overnight by courier and arrive first thing in the morning.

What has this idea got working for it? (That's Question 1.) Using a courier is cheaper than our normal delivery method, it's guaranteed overnight, the deadline is 6 pm and the courier has a depot nearby. Now for Question 2. What has this idea got working against it? The courier service is only guaranteed overnight to certain metropolitan areas, it is only good for small deliveries and it is not good for fragile items.

In this particular example, we only had one idea but it appears worth pursuing.

My company used this approach recently when we had to find a new office. We had six alternatives to choose from. We needed to sort them out and select the most promising one. We found that they all had things working for them and against them. Using this method, we decided on the office.

tools of the trade
Refer to Activity 19, Picking Winners, on page 142.

improving the odds
We have already discussed TLC as a way of showing your commitment. It is also a great way to improve the odds of your ideas being winners. It is a great way to take each potential idea and determine what needs to be fixed up or changed.

Remember, TLC stands for what is Tempting, Lacking or needs Changing in an idea:

▓ *Tempting.* What is tempting about this idea? What is the bit of magic in it? What looks good? Which bit do you like? What are some of the possibilities?

▓ *Lacking.* What is it lacking? What is missing? What does it need?

▓ *Changing.* What needs to be changed? What could be changed? What would make it better?

In our example of finding a new office, we used TLC to look closer at the High Street option:

▓ What was tempting about it? Its location, size, the amount of light upstairs, the rent, its availability and its 'feel' were all in its favour.

▓ What was lacking in it? It didn't have adequate storage, parking, ISDN lines or good light downstairs.

▓ What needed changing? It needed paint on walls, carpets, partitions, parking in the street, lease options.

It looked as though we could fix the things that were lacking or needed changing and improve it dramatically. So we made the necessary changes. We moved in and the office is working well for us.

If you encourage people to have lots of ideas at work, you will need to make good use of TLC. TLC helps you develop ideas further, to improve them and to fix up the bits that need it. It can help you take those one or two really good ideas and turn them into winners.

tools of the trade
Refer to Activity 20, Improving the Odds, on page 144.

seeing the finishing line
What would you do if you did pick a winner? What would you do if your 20 to 1 shot romped home? Imagine if you won the jackpot!

We have all imagined what would happen if we won something. We have all imagined ourselves on holiday, being promoted, making the sale or winning the lottery. Imagination is a powerful motivator. Imagination motivates people to climb mountains, to paint pictures and to win races. Imagination motivates people to keep their ideas alive and keep the energy going. Imagining what ideas will be like when they are finished is a vital part of the Action process.

The technique itself is very simple. All you need to do is imagine:

1. Grab a pen and some paper.
2. Imagine your idea finished, on the shelf, working perfectly.
3. Write the answers down to these questions:
    −   What does the idea look like now it is finished?
    −   What are people doing with it?
    −   What does it feel like to have developed a winning idea?
    −   What's a good picture or symbol for the finished idea?

The more clearly you can answer these questions, the more powerful the effect will be. I used this technique with a group once. We had a plan to restructure the entire organisation. It was going to be a huge task and there were going to be lots of barriers to overcome. Having a powerful image of what the new organisation would finally look like was going to be an important part of achieving it. It was a vital part of keeping everyone's enthusiasm going.

We also used this strategy in our high street office. We all visited the space before we leased it and had a good look around. We then grabbed a white board and some pens and imagined ourselves working there. We asked ourselves what it would look like, what it would feel like and what we liked about it. We developed a very strong concept about the finished office. It was now a simple matter of turning it into a reality.

tools of the trade
Refer to Activity 21, Seeing the Finishing Line, on page 146.

making it happen
It took the Wright brothers many attempts just to get off the ground. Their idea of 'heavier than air' flight took a while to get right. Lots of ordinary ideas are just as hard to get off the ground. They sometimes need 147 attempts before they fly on their own. Some never make it.

The problem is often due to the fact that it is hard to know exactly where to start and what to do next. It is one thing to have this great idea about flying. It is something else entirely to actually go and do it. It is one thing to dream of climbing a mountain. It is something else to actually start climbing.

To make it happen, I use a technique I call 'walking backwards'. Walking backwards does a number of positive things. It keeps your idea clearly in mind all the time, it keeps the enthusiasm going and it helps plan each step so you know exactly what to do next and where to start.

There are three steps in walking backwards:

1. Just imagine.
2. Take one step backwards.
3. Keep walking backwards.

step 1: just imagine
You have already done this in the previous stage. You already have a very clear sense of the finished product. You know exactly what your idea will look like and what it will do when it's finished.

step 2: take one step backwards
Ask yourself: 'What is the last thing I need to do to finish it off?

What was the last thing I needed to do to make it work?' In our holiday example, it would be to get off the plane. In our work example, it would be opening the door of the new offices on Monday morning.

step 3: keep walking backwards

Keep asking yourself: 'What did I do to make that happen?' In our holiday example, I had to get on the plane, to collect a ticket, to pay for the ticket, to decide where to go, to save money, to decide to take a break. In our work example we had to move the furniture in, lay the new carpet, paint the walls, get the wiring done, sign the lease, negotiate the lease, decide to move offices.

tools of the trade

Refer to Activity 22, Walking Backwards, on page 148.

I have seen many organisations that are full of ideas but are not very innovative. This is because having ideas is only part of the innovative process. Innovation is more than having the ideas. It is all about implementing ideas, developing them, refining them and acting on them.

Many organisations reject ideas far too soon. Ideas are seldom perfect when they are first conceived. They are embryonic and therefore need a lot of nurturing and development. Reject them too soon and a winning idea can get lost forever.

Acting is all about turning ideas into reality. Strategies like TLC and improving the odds can stop you throwing ideas away too soon and help you overcome some of the challenges you face in implementing them.

The IDEA Process helps people juggle ideas. It helps people think through the entire process – from having the thought, through to actually implementing it. It is a crucial part of the innovation process and is something that should become second nature to everyone involved in innovation.

So far we have only been juggling with three things – purpose, commitment and ideas. It is now time to add the fourth and final issue – the support required to keep innovation going and going.

juggling support

- the politics of innovation;
- best practice in innovation;
- vote 1 for innovation;
- juggling.

We now need to look at the final issue in the pursuit of innovation – juggling support.

the politics of innovation

You decide to take up politics. You have some good ideas about how things can be improved. You want to have a go at implementing those ideas. You know that you can make a difference. So you decide to stand as the new local member in the next election.

What happens next? Is it as simple as having the idea or do you need a few other things to make it happen? You bet you do!

Having a few good ideas and a 'will to win' has never got anyone elected. What gets people elected is a support system. They rely on what is behind them, what is backing them up, sustaining them and keeping them going. Most people get elected because of the 'party machine'. Think of the support that politicians enjoy. They will have a campaign headquarters full of keen volunteers. They will have media campaigns, promotional material, fundraising schemes, administrative support and a never-ending supply of helpers willing to do almost anything.

Where does all this initial support come from? It usually comes from people you already know. It usually comes from people who already know and support you in some way. It is these people you would start with, slowly getting their support and commitment. It is these people you have to convince that you have something to offer and that they should support you.

Once you have your 'friends' on side, you can start to build the support system you need to mount an effective campaign. Once you have your 'friends' on side, you can start to get support from the party machine. Only then do you start the serious job of getting support from the electorate, the people who will actually vote.

This gradual development of support happens long before anyone has cast a single vote, long before election day. When election day arrives, you might not be the one. Someone else might end up with more votes than you. Your dream of making a difference might remain just a dream.

Innovation is like trying to get elected. It is you and your ideas against the rest. And you will need all the help and support you can get.

In politics the best candidate does not always get elected – often it is the best-supported candidate. The party machine and the support it provides can make or break you. Innovation is the same. The marketplace is full of average ideas that have been launched and supported more effectively than some above-average ideas that never made it.

Innovation is about having great ideas, finding and developing support for those ideas, developing them to their fullest potential and positioning them so others find them irresistible.

If you want innovation to take root in your company and flourish, you will need to provide support.

ask the people

Elections are all about listening to the voice of the people and acting on it. Innovation is also about listening to the voice of the people and then acting on it. If you want to know what support people need to be innovative, then ask them. It sounds obvious – but often is not done effectively.

One way to do this is to use the technique known as 'stop, start and continue'. In 'stop, start and continue', you simply get a group of people together with a common goal in mind. You then ask them what, in order to achieve that goal, are the things that they should start doing, stop doing and continue doing. You end the meeting with three lists of ideas you can implement. And by asking people what they should start doing and continue doing, you avoid the negative mindset of what is stopping them and what is getting in the way, thereby creating a more positive mindset of what they can do and how they can make a difference.

To find out what should be done about innovation, get a group of people together and ask them what we should stop, start and continue doing to encourage innovation.

stop doing
Ask such questions as:

■ What is getting in the way?
■ What is stopping ideas from being implemented?
■ What is slowing the process down?

start doing
Ask such questions as:

■ What should we start to do?

- What can we do to have more ideas?
- What can we do to encourage others to have ideas?

continue doing
Ask such questions as:

- What are we currently doing that is working?
- What should we do more of?
- What is working?

best practice in innovation: what are others doing?

What follows are some of the things that companies around the world are doing to encourage and support innovation. Pick the ones that you feel fit best into your culture. Try them and see what happens. Be innovative.

1. director of innovation

One company I know created a new position – director of innovation, whose role was to drive innovation through the company. The job involved researching all the current thinking on innovation and how to encourage it, producing company newsletters, conducting creative thinking workshops, facilitating project groups, talking at conferences, running problem-solving sessions and taking every opportunity to promote innovation and new ideas.

The director of innovation also kept an eye on the competition and the market generally to see if there were any ideas that would be worth borrowing.

A person dedicated to innovation full-time is a great way to show support and commitment.

2. innovation champions

The company called for volunteers to be 'innovation champions', a job described as 'unpaid and additional to any normal duties'. Innovation champions were to provide help, support and advice to anyone who asked for it.

The company ended up with six people from different divisions. One had an accounting background, another was good at planning, a third was an expert in marketing, and so on. Everyone had a specific set of skills they could call upon. Their names and numbers were publicised so everyone in the company knew who to contact and how.

The idea was simple. If you had an idea and wanted some help with it, all you had to do was contact an innovation champion and support was there.

3. innovation booklet

This great idea was 40 pages of ideas, processes, pictures and reasons why everyone would benefit from innovation. It contained the company vision and how innovation was a vital part of the company's continued success. The booklet explained how and where anyone could get help and assistance for any worthwhile idea. It had creative problem-solving ideas and tips, processes to follow in getting ideas accepted and examples of how other ideas had succeeded.

The idea behind it was simple. If you want people to be innovative, you have to give them all the information they need. It has to be readily available and easy to use. Every person in the company got a copy. Every person in the company was encouraged to be as innovative as they possibly could be.

4. creative problem-solving workshops

I worked with an organisation that asked me to train every

single person in creative thinking skills. A series of one-day workshops focused on how to have and implement creative ideas. We called it 'Having great ideas'. Everyone attended; everyone was encouraged to come up with an idea and implement it.

We formed a number of 'innovation project teams'. Each team developed an idea that they worked through and implemented. The workshop covered such things as thinking 'outside the box', clarifying issues and coming up with alternatives, thinking about solutions and how to implement the best ones. Each project was monitored and its success measured.

5. measuring success

Just as there are many different types of innovation, there are also many different ways of measuring its success. At one extreme you can measure the financial cost of a single idea. At the other extreme you can determine how you are perceived in the market place. Some innovations, such as product innovations, are easier to measure and to put numbers to. Other innovations, such as people innovations that impact on the culture and climate of the organisation, are harder to measure.

Many organisations use a variety of measures. They measure the cost and return of each idea, at the same time tracking how long it takes ideas to make their way from concept to implementation. They also carry out both internal climate surveys and external customer surveys to gauge how different people perceive them. This mixture of measurement methods gives them a better picture of what is happening.

Some of the more common measurement methods include:

- ▨ Bottom line results
  - return on investment;
  - actual cost;
  - actual returns;
  - amount allocated to R&D;

- number of people involved;
- amount of time allocated.

■ Progress and performance
- number of ideas submitted;
- number of ideas implemented;
- progress of ideas through the system;
- time taken to get ideas into the market;
- risk/exposure involved in each idea.

■ Contribution and culture
- employee surveys;
- climate surveys;
- skills audit;
- amount of teamwork;
- levels of collaboration.

■ Perceptions and direction
- customer surveys;
- customer feedback;
- industry assessment;
- employee surveys;
- market perception;
- positioning.

I found that the most innovative companies do not leave it to chance. They have the processes and structures in place to encourage innovation at every opportunity. One of the best ways to get people to be innovative is to measure how well they do it. Include innovation in any performance systems you have. Make innovation an important part of every individual's job and measure them against it. Discuss it during any appraisal discussions you have with them.

6. the marketplace

Once a month the canteen was turned into a marketplace. Anyone with an idea was encouraged to bring it along and sell it. Each idea had its own display stand – the company would provide the stands and any materials needed to make it look good. The owner of the idea and any supporters it had would operate the stand.

The ideas committee would spend two hours walking around the marketplace looking, talking, asking questions and finding out all they could about each idea. The marketplace was designed to give every idea an equal chance of succeeding.

The ideas committee was made up of a number of people from the key functions within the organisation. It had someone from finance on it, to check the figures. It had someone with production experience, someone from marketing and someone from the human resources team. The committee could evaluate ideas from a number of perspectives. If the ideas committee 'bought' an idea, they would provide the resources needed to develop it into a full-blown innovation project for final approval by the management committee.

Better than most suggestion schemes, the marketplace gave everyone an equal chance to sell and explain their ideas. Every idea and person involved was recognised and rewarded in some way, whether or not they made it. And the entire process was an innovation in itself and showed the company's commitment to the process.

7. the banker

Have you ever needed to borrow money? Well, this was the banker you dream of! He had lots of money and his job was to give it away... interest free!

The management of the company would decide how much money it would spend developing ideas. So if you had an idea but lacked the funds to develop it, you could go to the banker and ask for some. If you could convince the banker that your idea was worth pursuing, you got what you needed.

You were judged on the success of your idea. The banker was judged on how much money he had rid himself of.

8. thinking space

Remember the question, 'Where are you when you get your best ideas?'. One company recognised the fact that thinking and working were often two different things. And to do them you needed two different places. To work, you needed a computer, a desk, a phone, fax machines, people and so on. To think, you needed a stimulating environment, no interruptions, room to move around in, relaxing music and, if possible, a view. They also recognised that thinking was as important as working, so they encouraged both activities.

Parts of the office were turned into thinking areas. They used to be meeting areas. The white walls were painted and covered with pictures. CD players were put in each room. Freshly ground coffee and fresh fruit were freely available. There were toys to play with, walls to draw on, websites to visit and books to look through.

Thinking was not only allowed but also encouraged.

9. 'what if...?'

You should now know all about using the 'What if...?' strategy. At Herrmann International every meeting we have has 'What if...?' on the agenda. We pick a topic and say, 'If this happened, what would we do?'. In customer service meetings we ask, 'What if we lost our best client?'. In administration meetings we ask, 'What if our computer network went down?'. In sales meetings we ask, 'What if the client doubles the order?'.

Sometimes we ask a positive question, sometimes a more negative one. But whatever the question is, it is encouraging all of us to anticipate, to be ahead of things, to think. And it only takes five minutes.

Put 'What if...?' on the agenda of every meeting.

10. the company memory

Have you ever had an idea, only to forget it? I often find I am in the wrong place at the wrong time. I will be shopping, driving, gardening or playing golf and an idea will pop into my head. Having lost a lifetime of ideas before now, I carry a little book and a pen everywhere. I jot my idea down and carry on. Then when I have time I can look it up and think about it some more.

Too many good ideas are lost before they have a chance to prove themselves. Some people sleep with a note pad by the bed. A friend of mine drives with Post-it notes at the ready.

Imagine a company with 100 people in it. How many thoughts and ideas would they all have in any one day? Imagine capturing all of those and being able to look through them and pick the best ones. Technology is great for capturing ideas and creating a 'company memory'. Have a bulletin board on your computer network where people can freely go. They can read what is there, add to it, laugh and make connections.

Like most memories, it will probably end up containing a lot of stuff that has little value. But amongst it all will be a few gems.

11. give people time

One company is famous for its 15 per cent rule, which says that some people are allowed to spend 15 per cent of their time thinking about and working on any creative ideas and projects. They do not have to ask anyone or get prior approval to do this. It is an unwritten rule to encourage innovation. Apparently it works. How much time do you give to people to think?

12. selection

I am told that if Bill Gates from Microsoft interviews you, he will ask, 'What is the biggest mistake you have ever made?'. I don't know about you, but if someone asked me that I would do my best to hide it, to change the subject and to focus on what I had done that worked. The last thing I would want to talk about are my mistakes.

Why does Bill Gates ask about mistakes? What is he trying to find out? He is trying to find out if you are a risk taker. He is actually not interested how many times you have screwed up. He is more interested in how many risks you have taken. Risk takers are good for innovation. Risk takers can be good for business.

Think of the last person you selected for a job. What part did 'mistakes they have made' play in your decision? If you are like the majority, then you chose someone who got it right more that they got it wrong. You might have selected someone who never takes a risk, who never steps out of line or who never goes it alone. That might be OK for business, but if innovation is what you are after, it might not be the best approach.

Ask yourself if you actively select for such things as:

- the ability to develop and hold a point of view;
- independent decision-making skills;
- initiative;
- networking skills;
- resilience and determination;
- enjoyment of achievement.

'We have to stop hiring people who are difficult to manage.' We were having a board meeting to discuss the future of a company for which I once worked. The Managing Director said those words. Everyone around the table agreed with them. Three years later the company sold out. I believe it was because of those words. We lost our position in the market. Our clients stopped buying from us, the company changed.

In hindsight the 'difficult to manage' were the very people we needed. Without them we lost our drive. They might be difficult to manage but you cannot do without them.

13. the big bang approach

I have worked with a few companies who liked the big bang approach to innovation. In each case we started with a two-day innovation conference.

Day 1 covered things like why we were doing this, the new company vision and direction and what place innovation would play in the future. It was then straight into creative thinking and learning how to think differently. The idea was to get people thinking 'outside the box'.

On Day 2 we split people into innovation project teams. They spent the day getting to know each other, learning how to work together and deciding on a project to work on.

The composition of the teams was vital. Each team was carefully selected to be as diverse as possible. Each team needed people from different parts of the company with different perspectives, different jobs, different skills and different ways of thinking. One of the most common reasons that teams find it hard to innovate is that they are made of like-minded people. It might help them get on with each other but it does little to help the creative process. Innovation and creative thinking thrive on difference.

Everyone left the conference all fired up and ready to implement an innovative project over the next few months. There was lots of follow-up and support for the teams as they went about their tasks. Six months later we all got together again and celebrated the successes.

The secret to the big bang approach is to keep it going. You might have to make the conference an annual event, selecting new people and new teams each time.

14. innovation project teams

You don't have to start with the big bang. Some companies still use the team approach, but in a low-key way. Instead of a big conference with lots of people and noise, you might just start with one or two teams. These could be formed at work. They could learn the necessary skills in short training sessions. They could quietly go about their work and implement their innovation projects at the same time. If you have the right sort of culture, go for the big bang approach. If not, quietly introduce innovation project teams.

15. networking and decisions

Many companies have a help desk. For example, if you are having problems with your computer you call the computer help desk and get an immediate answer. You might be a customer with a question about your account. You can call the help desk and have your query answered straight away. If only innovation was as simple as that! If only innovation was a matter of picking up the phone and getting help.

While innovation might not be a simple matter, many people still need help and assistance in making ideas happen. You might not be able to provide one help desk to solve all the problems but you need to do something. What you need to do is give people the skills and ability to get whatever help they need as and when they need it.

Networking is the modern word for 'knowing the right people'. I have a friend who always seems to know the 'right person' to turn to. From plumbers to accountants and from painters to car mechanics, ask him and he will give you a name. Networking is an important skill. It is something that can be taught to everyone.

For those who don't know the 'right people', you can use the help desk concept. Publicise the names and numbers of your innovation champions. Make sure everyone knows the director of innovation. Promote the fact that your door is always open to anyone who needs to talk through an idea or ask for assistance.

As to the actual skill of networking, some people seem to be born with it. They know everyone they need to know. Other people find it more challenging. So, why not include a segment on networking in any training you run? I spend two hours of a two-day creative thinking workshop specifically on how to network and get the support you need.

During these two hours I focus on a number of key characteristics of networks:

1. Networks occur naturally and everyone belongs to at least one. Think of your family as a network. Think of your friends as a network.
2. Networks generally exist around a common interest or purpose. They are sometimes referred to as 'communities of practice'. For example, model plane enthusiasts get together at weekends, people with an interest in acting form theatre groups and people with a common professional interest form associations. Inside organisations similar networks exist around common interests and purposes.
3. Networks tend to be non-hierarchical. They tend to grow across the organisation rather than down it. Everyone tends to be an equal, each making his or her own unique contribution to the network. They tend not to have formal rules and structures.
4. Networks tend to be based on a set of shared values. These generally include an openness and trust that encourages a high level of collaboration.

After discussing these features, I focus on some of the things that people do that seem to be important in being a good networker:

1. Make yourself available to others. When asked by anyone to help or assist, do so openly and willingly. This is vital, as most networks are built on mutual trust.
2. Listen to people talk about their networks and how they get help and assistance. Learn from them.
3. Ask for help when you need it. Ask co-workers rather than managers.
4. Become aware of the informal communication channels within the organisation. Networks are very effective at passing on information.
5. Join some professional associations inside or outside the organisation.
6. Find out what 'communities of practice' currently exist within the organisation. Find people who have similar interests to yours.
7. Check the organisation's management and information system to see what it has in it and how useful it might be.
8. Be good at remembering names and faces.

Another key skill is the ability to get the 'right' decision. It is one thing to know the 'right' person; it is something else to ensure they make the 'right' decision and give you the support you need. Getting favourable decisions is really a matter of selling your idea to someone so they will support it. One company I work with actually runs a programme called 'Making and getting decisions'. The programme teaches two key skills. The first is ensuring any decision you make is balanced and well thought through. This is decision making. The second skill, decision getting, is understanding how other people make decisions and what will influence them. Once you understand this, you can position your idea in a way that increases the chance of getting a 'yes'.

16. publicity

What about publishing a one-page innovation newsletter every month? One page makes it quick and easy to read. It also makes it quick and easy to write! Keep it simple. Produce lots of them and make sure everyone gets a copy. Back it up with more detailed material on the various projects or ideas that people have developed. Have a page on the computer network where people can go to read the latest news.

Other ideas I have seen include posters that promote the benefits of innovation and feature the 'Innovative employee of the month', a special page on the company intranet that has the very latest in innovative news and views and one CEO who never missed an opportunity to stress the importance of innovation and to get examples and recognition to anyone who had tried.

People like to be recognised and they like to know what is going on.

17. celebrations and rewards

The Oscars, the Golden Globe and Sportsman of the Year are all awards recognising achievement and celebrating success. And people love them. How does your company recognise its achievements and celebrate its successes?

Does it have an annual innovation award ceremony? Does it reward people financially? Does it give away non-financial rewards such as a holiday, dinners, trophies or other gifts?

Consider a cash bonus for each idea that gets to a certain stage in the process, or a holiday for the 'innovation of the year', a special award for the most innovative person elected by their peers, and so on. I worked with one company that had a 'Best idea of the year award'. The prize was a holiday for two to the Great Barrier Reef. Another organisation based their award ceremony on the Oscars, and had a full-blown awards night complete with invitations to partners. The trick is to be as innovative in the way you reward people and celebrate success as you are in coming up with ideas in the first place.

vote 1 for innovation

Organisations cannot rely on the 'creative few'. If organisations are serious about innovation, everyone needs to be involved, all the time. If you want everyone involved you need to provide a strong and effective support structure. You need a powerful party machine.

If you systematically work through these questions, you will go a long way to creating the support needed.

support checklist

question 1. who is responsible?
Is there one person who:

- is the champion of innovation?
- publicly commits to making it happen?
- can get the resources needed?
- will put their own time in to keep it going?

question 2. why do it?
Do your employees:

- know why innovation is important?
- know why it is vital for the business?
- know how it will help them?

question 3. what will it look like?
Do people:

- know what the vision is?

■ get excited about it?
■ know innovation when they see it?

question 4. who else needs to be involved?
Does everyone:

■ know how to get the support they need?
■ know how to network with others?
■ have the ability to get things done?

question 5. how will we do it?
Do people:

■ understand and value the difference and diversity that individual people bring?
■ understand the innovation process and what is involved?
■ have creative thinking and problem-solving skills?
■ know how to implement ideas and follow them through?
■ know how to be part of project teams?

question 6. how will you keep it going?
Do you know how you are going to:

■ measure it?
■ reward people for it?
■ recognise ongoing achievements?
■ link it with the other organisational systems?
■ make it part of everyday life – the way we do things?

tools of the trade
Refer to Worksheet 23, the Final Checklist, on page 150. Fill it in with your organisation in mind.

juggling

We began this book by comparing juggling with innovation. We looked at how juggling involves keeping your eyes on more than one thing at a time. It involves moving continuously and quickly. It involves making slight adjustments in the way you catch or throw the balls. It involves watching, moving, responding, adjusting, catching, throwing and concentrating. It also involves letting things go.

Juggling is dynamic. Juggle and you will never feel totally in control. Hopefully you can now see why I think innovation is a lot like juggling. Innovation is as dynamic as juggling is. Innovate and you will never feel totally in control.

People will juggle with almost anything – balls, bats, knives, firebrands and chainsaws get thrown around in an effort to demonstrate their skills and to distinguish themselves from others.

We now know that innovation is different. There are four things the innovator must juggle: purpose, commitment, ideas and support. Keep these 'in the air' and you will be well on the way to making innovation happen.

tools of the trade – activities and worksheets

- how innovation works;
- getting innovation started and The Idea Process;
- juggling support.

Like most people with a trade, I have built up quite a toolkit over the years. Some of them I use all the time, others I have only used once or twice. But I still carry them all with me, just in case.

What follows are some of the tools and techniques that I have found to be most useful. These are the ones I go armed with whenever I start working with people and organisations to make innovation happen. They are also the ones that I have referred to throughout this book.

I use them in a variety of ways. Sometimes I am working on my own. In that case I will use them to assist me in whatever I am trying to do. Other times I might be working with a group or team of people, helping them work through an issue. In this case I would use the same tools in a different way, acting as a facilitator and allowing others to work through the issue.

For each of the various tools and techniques I have included here, there are hints on how to use it yourself and how to facilitate others in using it. I hope you find them as useful as I have.

To make it a bit easier to find them, I have organised them under the same headings as the book's chapters.

how innovation works

The following exercises are good ones to make people aware of the opportunities for innovation. People often have a narrow definition of innovation, thinking that innovation is restricted to the production areas of the company. These exercises can broaden understanding of innovation and encourage people to look for opportunities of their own.

Have a go at completing them yourself first. Then get your team together and see what they come up with.

activity 1 – the four Ps

Use Worksheet 1 to explore these types of innovation existing in your organisation:

- ▨ procedural;
- ▨ people;
- ▨ process;
- ▨ product.

on your own

For each of the four types of innovation, write an example of innovation in your organisation. Review what you have written. Is your organisation equally good at all types of innovation? Is there room for improvement? If so, where?

Think about the opportunities that exist for being more innovative in other areas of the organisation.

with a group

Ask each individual to complete the worksheet by themselves first. Then get everyone to share their thoughts with the whole group. Capture the comments on a flipchart or a white board. Ask the group to agree on where the greatest opportunities exist. Try and agree on some action steps that people can take away and implement. Monitor the progress and see if you can spread innovation to other parts of the organisation.

worksheet 1 – the four Ps

Type of innovation   Example

Procedural

People

Process

Product

activity 2 – the triple jump

on your own

Think about the sorts of ideas that you, or your organisation, are good at coming up with. Think about the ideas you have had. Complete Worksheet 2 and decide where the greatest opportunities exist. What can you do to come up with other types of innovations?

with a group

Ask each individual to complete the worksheet by themselves first. Then get everyone to share their thoughts with the total group. Capture the comments on a flipchart. Ask the group to agree on where the greatest opportunities exist. Get the group to agree on some action steps to increase the level of innovations.

worksheet 2 – the triple jump

Triple jump   **Example**

Ideas that hop

Ideas that step

Ideas that jump

activity 3 – four Ps/triple jump combination

on your own
Complete Worksheet 3 and decide where the greatest challenges and opportunities exist.

Decide on what actions you can take.

with a group
Ask each individual to complete the worksheet by themselves first. Then get everyone to share their thoughts with the total group. Capture the comments on a flipchart. Ask the group to agree on where the greatest opportunities exist.

Get the group to decide what action steps they can take to increase the level of innovation.

worksheet 3 – four Ps/triple jump combination

	Innovation	Ideas that hop	Ideas that step	Ideas that jump
Procedural				
People				
Process				
Product				

getting innovation started

Once there is a general awareness of the need and the opportunities for innovation, the next step is to make everyone aware of the organisation's purpose.

juggling purpose

In some cases it is just a matter of communicating an existing purpose. In other cases it is a matter of creating a new one. Whichever one applies to your organisation, I find the whole subject of organisational purpose a great one to build a workshop or conference around.

activity 4 – organisational purpose

purpose
Gaining commitment to a common purpose.

on your own
You can use this worksheet on your own. I initially used it to think through the purpose of my organisation. But I soon involved other people as I realised the need for their commitment.

with a group
This exercise is always best done with a group. Commitment to a common purpose is such an important aspect of making innovation happen that it is too good an opportunity to miss. Get together the group you want to involve. Ask them to complete the exercise as individuals first. Then ask them to share their ideas and discuss them. Keep the discussion going until there is agreement about the purpose.

You might need to spread this over two or three meetings to allow enough time for people to think closely about it. Once you have agreed on a final purpose, test it against the four criteria: is it simple, memorable, magic and for everyone?

worksheet 4 – organisational purpose

What does the organisation actually do? (Does it manufacture a product? Sell something? Provide a service to people?)

Now ask yourself, 'Why do we do this?' Keep asking yourself 'why' until you reach your purpose:

1. 'Why do we do this?' To:

2. 'Why do we do this?' To:

3. 'Why do we do this?' To:

4. 'Why do we do this?' To:

5. 'Why do we do this?' To:

Review your final statement and work it into a statement of purpose that is simple, memorable, magic, for everyone.

juggling commitment

Commitment is something you give to other people. You do it by acting each and every day. Commitment must be maintained all the time, and it is often the little things that are important.

These next three worksheets can be used each day. They are quick and easy to use. They will show your commitment to thinking differently about things. Once you show such a commitment, others will follow.

Start by using them on issues you have to work on directly. Once you are familiar with them, use them with other people. Make them part of 'the way we do things around here'.

activity 5 – the ladder

purpose
For deciding the best level to start at.

on your own
Follow the instructions on the ladder to analyse the best place to start working on a particular issue.

with a group
Start with a clear definition of the issue. Start with the wording: 'In what way might we...', or 'How can we...', and allow five to 10 minutes for everyone to complete the ladder on their own. Then put people in small groups. Allow enough time for each group to agree on one ladder. Get each group to share their ladder with the others. Finally combine all the ladders into one. Agree on the best place or places to start innovations.

worksheet 5 – the ladder

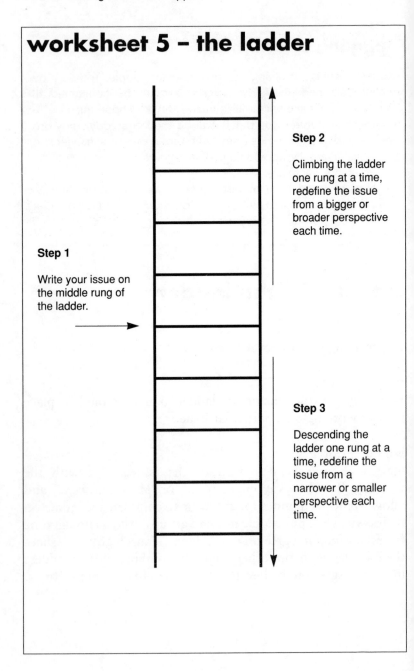

Step 2

Climbing the ladder one rung at a time, redefine the issue from a bigger or broader perspective each time.

Step 1

Write your issue on the middle rung of the ladder.

Step 3

Descending the ladder one rung at a time, redefine the issue from a narrower or smaller perspective each time.

activity 6 – 'what if...?'

on your own

Any time you want a new perspective or a fresh idea, think 'What if...?' Start each day with a few 'What ifs...?' about what might happen during the day. Just before you go into a meeting, ask yourself, 'What if...?' Make thinking 'What if...?' a natural part of your everyday thinking.

with a group

Include 'What if...?' on the agenda of all your meetings. Check decisions by asking 'What if...?' Use 'What if...?' at every opportunity to help people think ahead.

worksheet 6 – 'what if...?'

Think about the issue you are dealing with. Write it down:

Now ask some of the following questions:

What if it...

Got better?

Got worse?

Happened more often?

Never happened again?

Cost a lot more?

Was free?

Changed colour?

Rained?

Write down any thoughts that come to mind.

Now make up your own 'What if...?' questions.

What if it...

activity 7 – TLC

Whenever you hear about something new or different, give it a bit of TLC.

on your own
Use this worksheet to assess your ideas.

with a group
Gather the group together, overview the issue you are dealing with and get them to brainstorm around TLC. When they have answered all the questions, get them to agree on the actions that they will each take. This is a great way to decrease negativity around new ideas and to increase the commitment.

worksheet 7 – TLC

Select an idea you have come up with. See what a bit of TLC can do for it.

My idea is to:

What's tempting is:

What's lacking is:

What needs changing is:

Now look at your idea again. What does it look like now? Is it a winner? Can it be improved?

activity 8 – alighting organisational purpose

definition

Organisational purpose is a clear statement about what an organisation is doing and why.

with a group

This is always best done with a group of people. Get together the people you want to involve. Ask them to complete the exercise as individuals first. Then ask them to share their ideas and discuss them. Keep the discussion going until there is agreement about the purpose.

You might need to spread this process over two or three meetings to allow enough time for people to think closely about it. Once you have agreed on a final purpose, test it against the four criteria: is it simple, memorable, magic and for everyone?

worksheet 8 – alighting organisational purpose

Write down what it is that the organisation actually does. For example, does it manufacture a product, sell something or provide a service to people?

Now ask yourself, 'Why do we do this?' Keep asking yourself 'why' until you reach your purpose.

1. 'Why do we do this?' To:

2. 'Why do we do this?' To:

3. 'Why do we do this?' To:

4. 'Why do we do this?' To:

5. 'Why do we do this?' To:

Review your final statement and work it into a statement of purpose that is simple, memorable, magic and for everyone.

activity 9 – alighting individual purpose

Use this worksheet to develop a sense of purpose yourself. What is it that you enjoy and why? What gives you the greatest sense of achievement and why? Spend some time on your own working through these questions. You might have to go back over it a few times before the answers come.

worksheet 9a – alighting individual purpose

Write down what it is that you actually do. What is it you enjoy doing? What turns you on at work?

Now ask yourself, 'Why do we do this?' Keep asking yourself 'why' until you reach your purpose:

1. 'Why do we do this?' To:

2. 'Why do we do this?' To:

3. 'Why do we do this?' To:

4. 'Why do we do this?' To:

5. 'Why do we do this?' To:

You should now be very close to your purpose – to what it is that drives you and makes you do the things you do. Being focused like this can really help you achieve things.

worksheet 9b – helping others find purpose

Use this worksheet to help others develop a sense of purpose. What is it that they enjoy and why? What gives them the greatest sense of achievement and why?

Allow them some time on their own working through these questions. They might have to go back over it a few times before the answers come.

Write down what it is that you actually do. What is it you enjoy doing? What turns you on at work?

Now ask yourself, 'Why do we do this?'. Keep asking yourself 'why' until you reach your purpose:

1. 'Why do we do this?' To:

2. 'Why do we do this?' To:

3. 'Why do we do this?' To:

4. 'Why do we do this?' To:

5. 'Why do we do this?' To:

You should now be very close to your purpose – to what it is that drives you and makes you do the things you do. Being focused like this can really help you achieve things.

activity 10 – alighting team purpose

purpose
Use this worksheet when helping teams develop a sense of purpose. Use it to find out why the team exists, what it is the team is trying to achieve and why.

with a group
Involve everyone in the task of working through the questions and developing the team purpose. The more involvement, the greater the commitment.

worksheet 10 – alighting team purpose

Write down what the team actually does. Why has the team been formed?

Now ask yourself, 'Why do we do this?' Keep asking yourself 'why' until you reach your purpose.

1. 'Why do we do this?' To:

2. 'Why do we do this?' To:

3. 'Why do we do this?' To:

4. 'Why do we do this?' To:

5. 'Why do we do this?' To:

You should now be very close to your team purpose – to what it is that drives you and makes you do the things you do. Being focused like this can help the team achieve things.

activity 11 - the aligning process

Aligning is an ongoing process. Take every opportunity you can to align people to the organisation's purpose. You can do this in formal meetings, in one-to-one discussions and any time you assign tasks and talk about performance.

To align people, use the following steps:

Step 1: tell everyone the organisation's purpose. Make sure everyone understands the organisation's purpose and why it is important.

Step 2: help people develop a sense of individual purpose. Use the process discussed under Alighting: Developing Individual Purpose.

Step 3: discuss how both can achieve their purpose. Discuss how both parties can achieve their purpose. Look for areas of overlap. Develop these further. Look for areas of 'underlap' and discuss ways of dealing with this.

---

juggling ideas

Innovation means having more ideas than you know what to do with. It is also about working with those ideas and shaping them the way you want to. You can juggle ideas on your own or in groups with others. You can use any of the techniques below in either way.

initiating The IDEA Process

Anticipating the future, being one step ahead of the market, solving small problems before they become big ones, creating new opportunities, out-thinking the competition, designing innovative products, being ahead of the game, being first, setting the pace, creating the future.

activity 12 – 'what if...?'

on your own
Any time you want a new perspective or a fresh idea, think
'What if...?' Start each day with a few 'What ifs...?' about
what might happen during the day. Just before you go into a
meeting, ask yourself 'What if...?' Make thinking 'What if...?'
a natural part of your everyday thinking.

with a group
Include 'What if...?' on the agenda of all your meetings. Check
decisions by asking 'What if...?'. Use 'What if...?' at every
opportunity, to help people think ahead.

worksheet 12 – 'what if...?'

Think about the issue you are dealing with. Write it down.

Now ask some of the following questions:

What if it...

Got better?

Got worse?

Happened more often?

Never happened again?

Cost a lot more?

Was free?

Changed colour?

Rained?

Write down any thoughts that come to mind.

Now make up your own 'What if...?' questions.

What if it...

activity 13 – long jumping

on your own
Simply work through the process on your own and see what thoughts and ideas you have.

with a group
This is a great technique to use at the annual planning or strategy meeting. You can use it to anticipate the future and to decide what the company will have to look like if it is to thrive. You can also use it on a more specific issue such as a single product or service.

worksheet 13 – long jumping

Select something you want to wonder about and a time to do it in.

I wonder what _____ will be like in the year _____?

Take three steps backwards: pick three dates in history.

Date 1:

Date 2:

Date 3:

For each of the dates you have selected, describe as best as you can what it would have been like then.

Date 1:

Date 2:

Date 3:

Jump. Now describe what it will be like in the future date you selected.

Date:

Finally, if things are going to be the way you described them, what are some of the things you are going to have to do in order to do what you want to?

defining

Defining the issue: dealing with the right issue at the right level, having many points of view, having lots of problems to work on, being spot on, dealing with the cause, setting yourself up for creative solutions, having many, yet different, descriptions of problems, seeing problems positively.

activity 14 – Who Do What

purpose
This is good for defining issues and deciding the best way to tackle things.

on your own
Simply work through the worksheet.

with a group
Get everyone working together to come up with as many ideas as possible. It can be a great exercise to get the ideas flowing.

worksheet 14 – Who Do What

Select a problem or issue you want to work on. Rephrase it by starting with the words 'How can I…'.

How can I...

Fill in each column in the Who Do What matrix.
Remember, work down each column, not across:

How can:	Who	Do	What
How can:			
How can:			
How can:			
How can:			
How can:			
How can:			

Randomly select any combination from the three columns and see what you come up with. Keep going until you have exhausted every combination.

activity 15 – the ladder workshop

purpose
For deciding the best level to start at.

on your own
Follow the instructions on the ladder to analyse the best place to start working on a particular issue.

with a group
Start with a clear definition of the issue. Start with the wording 'In what way might we...', or 'How can we...'. Allow five to 10 minutes for everyone to complete the ladder on their own. Then put people in small groups. Allow enough time for each group to agree on one ladder. Get each group to share their ladder with the others. Finally combine all the ladders into one. Agree on the best place or places to start.

Now decide which definition, or definitions will give you the best outcomes. Start working with those.

exploring

Exploring: having lots of ideas, solutions and perspectives, listening to intuition and insight, building ideas on ideas, selecting interesting ideas, keeping your thoughts together, brainstorming, daydreaming and think tanks.

worksheet 15 – the ladder

Step 2

Climbing the ladder one rung at a time, redefine the issue from a bigger or broader perspective each time.

Step 1

Write your issue on the middle rung of the ladder.

Step 3

Descending the ladder one rung at a time, redefine the issue from a narrower or smaller perspective each time.

activity 16 – brainstorming

You can brainstorm on your own but it is always best with a room full of people. Get your group together, give them lots of paper, pens and an issue to work with and let them loose. Keep the energy up and the enthusiasm going. Ten minutes of brainstorming can often give you more ideas that you will know what to do with.

Brainstorming can be used on almost any issue.

worksheet 16 – brainstorming

Write down the problem or issue you are exploring:

Now write down, as fast as you can, 20 ideas to solve it:

1.	11.
2.	12.
3.	13.
4.	14.
5.	15.
6.	16.
7.	17.
8.	18.
9.	19.
10.	20.

While you are doing this, look around the room, look out of the window, think about the outside world – make as many connections as you can!

Now think of 10 more ideas that are a little bit crazy:

1.	6.
2.	7.
3.	8.
4.	9.
5.	10.

Write down 10 ideas that you know will *not* work:

1.	6.
2.	7.
3.	8.
4.	9.
5.	10.

Now have a look over all the ideas you have written down. Highlight any that look interesting. Write the 10 'best' ideas down here:

1.	6.
2.	7.
3.	8.
4.	9.
5.	10.

Try combining some of them and see what you get.

activity 17 – mixing metaphors

on your own
Find yourself somewhere with a bit of peace and quiet. Work your way through the worksheet and see what comes to mind.

with a group
Start by getting each individual to work through it on their own. Once they have done that, put them in small groups to share their ideas and develop more. You can then combine all the ideas into one:

Step 1. Have something in mind that you want ideas about.

Step 2. Pick an object – chair, table, tree.

Step 3. List all the characteristics of the object.

Step 4. Stop and think about each characteristic in turn. Do they give you any ideas? List down the ideas you get.

Step 5. When you have run out of ideas, pick another object and start again. Keep going until you have lots of ideas.

Step 6. Look at all your ideas and see what you have!

worksheet 17 – mixing metaphors

Have something in mind that you want ideas about.

Pick a metaphor, like a zoo, a circus, a garden or a train.

List all the characteristics of the object you have picked.

Stop and think about each characteristic in turn. Do they give you any ideas? List the ideas.

When you have run out of ideas, pick another object and start again. Keep going till you have lots of ideas. Look at all your ideas and see what you have!

activity 18 – dicey ideas

on your own
Find yourself somewhere with a bit of peace and quiet. Work your way through the worksheet and see what comes to mind.

with a group
Start by getting each individual to work through it on their own. Once they have done that put them in small groups to share their ideas and develop more. You can then combine all the ideas into one.

worksheet 18 – dicey ideas

Pick an issue that you want to have a great idea about:

Step 1. Break your task into as many separate aspects as you can.

Step 2. From this list pick three that look good:

1.

2.

3.

Step 3. Think of six options for each topic:

Topic	Topic	Topic
1.	1.	1.
2.	2.	2.
3.	3.	3.
4.	4.	4.
5.	5.	5.
6.	6.	6.

Roll the dice again and again until you come up with some great ideas.

acting

Acting is a four-step process:

- ▓ picking winners;
- ▓ improving the odds;
- ▓ seeing the finish line;
- ▓ making it happen.

You can use these four steps on your own or with a group. The process is exactly the same.

activity 19 – picking winners

Write down each idea at the top of a piece of paper or use the worksheet. Then answer the two questions:

1. What does this idea have working for it?
2. What does this idea have working against it?

worksheet 19 – picking winners

Idea:_____

What does this idea have working for it?

What does this idea have working against it?

How do the pros and cons of this idea weigh up?

activity 20 – improving the odds

Take each idea in turn. See what it has working for it. How tempting does that make it? Now look at what you wrote down that is working against it. List these down under 'What's lacking'. Take each thing that is lacking in turn and see what you can change to improve that aspect of it.

Select an idea you have come up with. See what a bit of TLC can do to it.

worksheet 20 – improving the odds

My idea is to:

What's tempting is:

What's lacking is:

What needs changing is:

Now look at your idea again. What does it look like now? Is it a winner? Can it be improved?

activity 21 – seeing the finishing line

on your own
Find somewhere where you will not be disturbed for a while. Sit down, relax and imagine your idea finished, on the shelf and working perfectly. Using your imagination, think about the questions in the worksheet.

with a group
If you are working in a group, get them together for half an hour. Ask them to relax and think about the finished project. Get them to answer the questions on their own, then as a group.

worksheet 21 – seeing the finishing line

What does the idea look like now it is finished?

Describe what people would be doing with it.

What does it feel like to have developed a winning idea?

Draw a picture or symbol of the finished idea.

activity 22 – walking backwards

There are three steps in the walking backwards activity:

1. Just imagine.
You have already done this in the previous stage. You already have a very clear sense of the finished product. You know exactly what your idea will look like and what it will do when it's finished.
2. Take one step backwards.
Ask yourself: 'What was the last thing I needed to do to finish it off?', 'What was the last thing I needed to do to make it work?'
3. Keep walking backwards.
Keep asking yourself: 'What did I do to make that happen?'

juggling support

Innovation needs to be 'the way we do things around here'. It needs to be built into the policies and procedures. It needs to be helped along at every turn.

activity 23 – politics of innovation workshop

This is the final worksheet, and probably the most important one of all. Like most of the worksheets, you can use it in two ways. The first way is on your own, the second is with others. I always try to involve others in everything I do as it is the best way I know to show commitment.

I use this as the starting point for all the work I do with innovation. I might modify it a bit depending upon the organisation, but the approach is always the same.

However you decide to make innovation happen in your organisation, this is a great place to start.

worksheet 23 – final checklist

▧ Question 1: Who is responsible? Is there one person who:
   - is the champion of innovation?
   - publicly commits to making it happen?
   - can get the resources needed?
   - will put their own time in to keep it going?
▧ Question 2: Why do it? Do your employees:
   - know why innovation is important?
   - know why it is vital for the business?
   - know how it will help them?
▧ Question 3: What will it look like? Do people:
   - know what the vision is?
   - get excited about it?
   - know innovation when they see it?
▧ Question 4: Who else needs to be involved? Does everyone:
   - know how to get the support they need?
   - know how to network with others?
   - have the ability to get things done?
▧ Question 5: How will we do it? Do people:
   - understand and value the difference and diversity that individual people bring?
   - understand the innovation process and what is involved?
   - have creative-thinking and problem-solving skills?
   - know how to implement ideas and follow them through?
   - know how to be part of project teams?
▧ Question 6: How will you keep it going? How are you going to:
   - measure it?
   - reward people for it?
   - recognise the ongoing achievements?
   - link it with the other organisational systems?
   - make it part of everyday life – the way we do things?

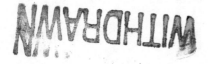